CW00435188

ONE S
Contracts

The One Stop Series

Series editor: David Martin, FCIS, FIPD, FCB
　　　　　　　Buddenbrook Consultancy

A series of practical, user-friendly yet authoritative titles designed to provide a one stop guide to key topics in business administration.

Other books in the series to date include:

David Martin　　　*One Stop Company Secretary*

David Martin　　　*One Stop Personnel*

Jeremy Stranks　　*One Stop Health and Safety*

ONE STOP
Contracts

JOHN WYBORN

ICSA Publishing
The Official Publishing Company of
The Institute of Chartered Secretaries and Administrators

First published 1996 by
ICSA Publishing Limited
Campus 400, Maylands Avenue
Hemel Hempstead
Hertfordshire, HP2 7EZ

Typeset in 10/11pt Sabon with Franklin Gothic by
Hands Fotoset, Leicester

Printed and bound in Great Britain by
T J Press (Padstow) Ltd

British Library Cataloguing in Publication Data

A catalogue record for this book is available from
The British Library

ISBN 1-872860-95-8

1   2   3   4   5   00   99   98   97   96

Contents

About the author   vii

Preface   ix

Acknowledgements   xi

1 **Surveying the scene and taking control**   1

2 **Knowing contract law**   21

3 **Drafting contracts**   37

4 **Standard contracts: the 'boiler plate' clauses**   51

5 **Procurement matters**   65

6 **Managing risks**   84

7 **Techniques of negotiating**   98

8 **Sales of goods and services; outsourcing**   109

9 **Agency**   124

10 **Intellectual property**   134

11 **Conclusions**   150

   Appendix: Contracts management and the company secretary:
      a 'health warning'   152

   Bibliography   154

   Index   155

About the Author

John Wyborn began his career in accountancy and organisation & methods. Entering the computer industry with Honeywell in the 1960s, he later joined Scicon, the BP-owned computer systems house, where he became successively consultant, then managing consultant, and then contracts manager. In 1986 he was also appointed company secretary. Throughout the 1980s he was directly responsible for the company's contracts administration, which included Ministry of Defence as well as civil contracting.

When BP disposed of Scicon to the Systems Designers Group in 1988 John stayed on, ultimately becoming assistant company secretary to SD-Scicon Plc. Following that Group's acquisition in 1991 by Electronic Data Systems Corporation of Dallas, Texas (EDS), part of the General Motors Organization, John took over the company secretaryship of the EDS registered companies in the UK. He left the group in 1993 to form his own consultancy, Craigwell Associates Ltd of Berkhamsted, Herts.

John is a member of the Institute of Management, the British Computer Society, and the Company Secretaries Group of the Institute of Chartered Secretaries and Administrators. He is also a council member of the Flint Organization, an association of independent computer specialists. He occasionally contributes to *The Company Secretary's Review*, and he lectures in London on contracts and company secretarial matters.

Preface

The management and administration of the contracts function for an organisation is a key commercial task. It implies responsibility for most of the legal relationships that the entity engages in with its customers, suppliers and others with whom it does business.

The successful contracts administrator has to know the enterprise, its staff and its structures. He or she has to know the law; to be able to set up controls which are effective without being restrictive; to understand people and their motivation; to have customer awareness; to be able to negotiate both with other organisations and with his own company, and to have not only general commercial knowledge but a high degree of old-fashioned common sense.

The aim of this book is to assist the contracts administrator who finds himself 'thrown in at the deep end', as it were. It is hoped that he might be able to take it home with him on a Friday night, study it over the weekend, and appear on the Monday morning with a reasonably clear idea as to what to do first, and in due course how to take it a lot further.

This book does not attempt to cover project management – which is a subject in itself – nor does it claim to be a complete legal reference book. Anyone following the main subjects: defining the task, taking control, the law and drafting of sales contracts, procurement, understanding risk management, should be able to make a significant contribution at once to the commercial stability of the undertaking. The ancillary topics such as agency, sales of goods and services, provide the building blocks of a developed contracts administration function. No one in this field can be truly operational without at least a small reference library, and at the end of the text is a short list of the books I have found helpful over the years.

Many of the more successful contracts specialists I have worked with have not been lawyers. They have been specialists in the fields of business in which they operate. This enables them to relate quickly to the commercial situations which confront them, and with the minimum of fuss to relate those situations to the law and its frameworks. Such people should always be prepared to fall back upon specialised professional help when they need it, especially when the risk factors are high. This book does not claim to provide that help so much as to give an indication of when and where to go to get it. It also tries to help them recognise risk when they see it.

Much of the material and ideas have been collated over the years from my work within the Scicon organisation, later SD-Scicon, and more recently within EDS in the United Kingdom, to whom I am indebted for much practical help and encouragement. In particular, they have permitted me to reproduce some of their standard contract clauses for analysis, and have provided material and ideas on outsourcing.

It is hoped that all of this material will now be of use to others.

John Wyborn
January 1996

Acknowledgements

In a book containing ideas and practical hints collected over some 20 years it is hard to know where to stop in framing acknowledgements.

First, appreciation is due to my friend and colleague David Martin, editor of this series, for suggesting that I write this book and for giving much practical advice. Within EDS I am much obliged to Mark Curtis, Tom Roy, Maurice Resnick, Richard Hawtin and others for their assistance and for giving me permission to quote from selected documentation.

Further back in time I should express my appreciation to Jon Mellor, Peter Lloyd, Bill Duperouzel and many other colleagues within the Scicon organisation of the 1970s and 1980s. Not only did they from time to time throw me into the deep end of contracts administration – arguably the best way of learning – but by displaying confidence in my ability to swim and offering essential support when I needed it, provided much of the material for this book!

1
Surveying the scene and taking control

Surveying the scene

It is the first day of our new role as contracts manager or administrator. Let us assume nothing. In that way we can review all of the points in turn. In smaller companies it is not unknown to find that we are the first to take on this task, the need for which may have been dimly recognised but never actually implemented until now.

Clarifying objectives

First of all, what it is that we are being asked to do? Definitions of 'contracts management' may include

- responsibility for checking and signing all contracts, or
- responsibility for managing all the company's contracts, or
- responsibility for ensuring that all the company's contracts are properly managed and completed on time and within budget, or
- responsibility for ensuring that all the company's commercial undertakings with third parties are conducted on a sound legal and/or commercial basis.

Quite clearly, these definitions differ widely in their scope and in the effort and skills needed to execute them. What is involved in each definition is going to vary between, say, a supplier of standard parts to the engineering industry, a mail order service, and a computer systems house with time and materials contracts, software licences, and large fixed price government contracts involving unusual skills, sub-contractors and high indemnity levels.

We are going to assume here that we are not expected to exercise day-to-day project management skills, which after all would justify a separate book in itself. Nor are we going to write ourselves down as mere contracts drafters, checkers and signers-off, though this is certainly a part of the work we shall do. As a working guide we might take the following definition as a hypothesis:

> The contracts manager is responsible for ensuring that all the company's contractual undertakings with third parties are conducted on a sound legal and/or commercial basis.

What is vital, however, is that each of us establishes what is right in our own organisation, in the very early stages. We might subject it to the PRAMKU test before we begin.

The PRAMKU test

P Are the objectives we are being set sufficiently *Precise?* ('Handle all the contracts for us, please'). That will hardly be enough.

R Are they *Realistic*? ('You will have to draft all the contracts. We've got about 20 contracts in progress. You will attend each monthly progress meeting, of course, which lasts about a day, and do the minutes, but don't forget the Board Meeting every other Tuesday'). If we accept this, we shall hardly have time to eat.

A Are they *Acceptable*? ('In this company we believe in Empowerment. You will be given an entirely free hand in everything to do with contracts, and so you will have the motivation of total responsibility'.) Are they paying us to be Chief Executive as well?

M Are they *Measurable*? ('On average we shall expect your unit to process one contract every 2.5 person/hours'.) A meaningless objective.

K Are they *Known*? ('Harry's been doing the job up to now, but between ourselves he's not very good at it. Just tell him I've asked you to take over, and by the way you can have his office which will give you a bit more room'.) A prescription for anxiety. Who will get axed next?

U Are they *Understood*? ('Frankly, the Chairman's not too sure about all this. We've never had a contracts specialist before; that's why there has been no announcement about your extra responsibilities. But he's sure there is a job to be done. Be a good soul and *make a start on it*'.)

'Making a start on it' can mean forgetting all preconceived notions, getting out of the office and finding out just what is happening. To use a term recently fashionable, it can involve 'management by walking about'. If no one else is going to write an acceptable scope of work, we shall need to construct one for ourselves. Here is one place to start – the sales ledger.

Examining the sales ledger

In most entities the sales ledger will show us those organisations with whom we are doing or have done business as a supplier of goods, services, rights or possibly expertise.

- Who in the company enters into commitments with these outside entities?
- Where are those people physically, and where in the organisation? To whom do they report?
- How much authority has been given to them to commit the organisation? How much authority do they themselves reckon they've got? Do the two versions agree?
- Are there written commitments, perhaps in the form of sales orders or other kinds of contract? Do we have copies, and where are they kept? Are they

signed by the other party, or are they merely an office record of salesmen's undertakings?

- Does anyone ever make verbal arrangements with customers? How are these afterwards dealt with? Are they later confirmed in writing in some way, or merely acted upon by mutual consent?
- How about amendments to sales orders, and extensions to agreements? Is there a procedure for assessing or agreeing to them, or is it mainly informal?
- Do we have standard contracts or terms and conditions, or do we accept other people's? And if we do, does anyone examine them first?
- Are there strict deadlines we have to meet which are essential to our customers, such as with Christmas or other seasonal goods, or 'milestones' to be reached in long term contracts involving stage payments?
- What are the penalties if we fail to meet these deadlines? Do we ever fail to meet them, or are our lines always available from stock?
- When we discuss amendments or extensions (sometimes termed 'variation orders' or 'v.o.'s') do we take into account their direct or indirect effect upon other deadlines to which we may be committed , some of which may have nothing to do with that project itself?
- Is there, indeed, any discussion of amendments at all, or do we merely accept them to keep the customer happy?

Examining the sales staff

Turning to our colleagues in the sales department who commit us to our customers, does the basis of their salary or reward support or conflict with the need to contract with integrity to ensure only sound business is accepted?

Are any of the sales staff paid on commission, for instance, and if so are there checks and balances to limit or moderate their authority?

New sales contracts – an early warning system

We have looked at the sales ledger now, and we have begun to ask ourselves some key questions about how commitments are entered into. Yet this is only part of the story. It refers to existing and past customers and contracts. Before we can be truly in control, we have to be in at the very beginning. How do we achieve this?

The answer may lie in 'hitching a lift' on some of the data which our sales organisation itself uses for internal management. Most sales staff are given targets. Most are required to report upon their prospective customers, either in the form of weekly call reports or else in discussion reports on sales meetings. A fully managed sales operation will have the need to record this data, to forecast 'chances of success', frequently in the form of percentages, and to predict likely decision dates and volumes or quantities of business expected.

Using the 'win' reports

Usually the sales staff themselves will be prompt enough to report 'wins', and the sales management will not be slow to update their records either. A contracts unit should seek access to this data. We need early warning of likely 'wins', when the jobs are likely to start, and what kind of jobs they are, in order to predict the kind of sales agreement needed, or the likelihood of protracted negotiations; and the likely elapsed time between expected 'wins' and the dates upon which the work has to be committed.

This information enables us to plan our workload, and also prevents premature commitment. One of the greater dangers in organisations arises when a sales team exerts pressure for the production or execution of an order 'because the customer cannot wait', while all the time that customer is not legally bound and can lawfully withdraw without penalty.

Watch out for 'letters of intent'

Letters of intent can be dangerous, since often they do not commit the buyer to buy. There are ways of responding to mere letters of intent, however, which allow interim activity to commence safely, and we shall deal with these in later chapters. The important thing, however, is that both sales and contracts people understand and implement these procedures, and use 'pressure of time' as a positive and not a negative bargaining counter. This needs mutual trust, and a realisation that successful commercial practice is to produce

---

Sound business, and not business at any price.

Might this, by the way, become our 'mission statement' (assuming of course that the Chairman can be persuaded that he thought of it first)?

Standard terms and conditions for standard items

We may find we are selling mainly stock or standard items, which might make our task a little easier. The essence of control here might be to ensure that standard conditions of sale, legally checked, are always used, that known time constraints which the customer may have, or 'time of the essence' clauses which he expressly places on us, are only accepted *after* checking with the warehouse and that, in these perilous times, *credit status* is regularly reviewed.

Take control of new job starts

One final step in ensuring contracts control of the sales operation may be to insist upon clearance by the contracts unit of all new works orders, warehouse despatches, or job instructions before their release. How big a task this might be will vary a great deal. If it appears onerous, consider applying some simple management expedients:

● Exempt all 'standard' situations, when they have been defined.

- Exempt all commitments below a certain value (provided there are no latent risks in the contract terms).
- Consider random or spot checks.
- Apply the '20/80' rule where appropriate. Concentrate upon clearance of those 20% of situations which may create 80% of the losses or other dislocations.
- Apportion *risk factors*, and scrutinise more closely those contracts with the highest factor levels.

Risk factor analysis can be one of the most potent of contracts management tools since it involves analysing what sets of circumstances make work risky in this organisation in particular, and devoting most management and contractual attention to them. As we shall discuss, many risky contracts can have the risks curtailed or eliminated at the negotiating stage, often with the counterparty's full knowledge and cooperation. This does need research and some knowledge available to us, which we may not have on Day One, however. Suffice it to say at this point that

---

The value or size of job can be a poor indicator of risk.

Other factors permitting, a firm of wholesale stationers might find it far less risky to supply £0.5 million worth of paper clips and staple guns to a large retail chain than £50,000 worth of personal computers with supporting business software.

Remember purchasing

The fact that much of the urgent, high-profile contracts activity exists between the sales department of a company and its customers should not blind us to the fact that an equal area of concern and potential risk lies within purchasing or procurement. Many organisations have a separate buying department which handles all of this. Ours, however, does not, so what should we do about it? First, remember:

Purchase orders are contracts too!

- Do we have purchase orders?
- Are they printed with all the correct Companies Act references?
- Is there a set of professionally drafted or checked terms and conditions on the back? If they are indeed on the back, are they readable or are they in pale grey 4 point microtype in the hope that no one will bother? And is there a notice on the front directing the reader's attention boldly to them, or is that in grey microtype too?

- Who is allowed to sign purchase orders?
- Where are blank purchase orders kept? Are they secure? Blank purchase orders are a little like blank cheques. Are they numbered like cheques and accounted for?
- Are suppliers instructed to quote these numbers on despatch documents and invoices, for recognition?
- Is there a process of marrying incoming payable invoices with the orders, marking down the orders to prevent duplicate supplies being received and paid for?
- Do we clear payable invoices in time to collect prompt payment discounts and such like?
- Is there a check upon quantity and quality of incoming goods and other materials?
- What proportion of payable invoices or payment requisitions get through the system for payment other than with purchase order support?
- Are these payments restricted to 'special situations' like legal or accountancy fees, Companies House fees, rents or public utility accounts, or is there widespread avoidance of the purchase order process?
- If there is, how easy would it be to enlist suppliers' cooperation by indicating that settlement will be delayed whenever order numbers are not quoted?

Beware in particular of printing, publishing, public relations, art work and other 'creative' activities where for quite sound operational reasons orders may be given in general terms and over the telephone. Invoices may subsequently be late in arriving and become hard to allocate. Whenever this happens, enquire who has the authority to order verbally, whether the supplier knows this and knows that no other person has any such ostensible authority. Ask whether confirming orders in writing are *always* sent within a given period of no more than a few days, *with copies elsewhere in the company.*

- How about the system for requisitioning or requesting purchase orders?
- Is it linked to budgets and budget signing authority, or can anyone have a go if the buyer knows them?
- Is the buyer required to seek alternative quotations? Does he or she influence the source?
- What procedures exist to discourage collusion? Is more than one unconnected person involved in the buying process? By 'unconnected' we mean 'answerable to different bosses'.
- Are there policies for periodic competitive tendering where it has become expedient to award repeat business on closed tender, year after year, to preferred suppliers 'because they know our business'?

It may be objected that much of this forms part of the normal audit trail of any company keeping proper books of account, and with competent auditors, either internal or external. It is, however, always worth a little enquiry especially when we are seeking to define or clarify where the contracts control function should start or end.

Examine the special situations

Having formed a view of the more repetitive or structured procurement processes, let us examine the special situations. One class of purchasing which will concern us directly, if it exists, is that of procuring supplies or services specifically to fulfil part of a customer or supplier contract. This might, for instance, form part of a government supply contract. We may, as a prime contractor, be required to undertake a great many responsibilities on behalf of our supplier.

This is no longer a matter of standard purchase orders. It often becomes a question of passing down, with a little redrafting, considerable and lengthy passages in a prime tender document to one or more suppliers, requiring them to submit prices and other responses indicating acceptance of all the 'small print' and quite a few of the deadlines for execution, each in respect of separate work packages which form a part of the whole for which we ourselves are tendering. Often this calls for many meetings both with the suppliers and with the prospective customer, so that a hierarchy of prices is arrived at to support our own tender.

Are there any collaboration agreements or joint ventures to be set up or administered? If so, to what extent are they hierarchical, and to what extent are they managed by steering committee or consent (this is always a difficult area).

Allow time for bargaining or preparation

Collaborative processes may involve weeks or months of work before tenders are submitted, and possibly more contractual work for several weeks after a tender is won. Bid bonds and other documents of guarantee are sometimes required. In such cases a contracts or commercial assistant may be working full time with the bid team for quite a while. Do we have any of these prospects on the horizon, and are we able to staff our unit accordingly? Bargaining takes time!

Intellectual property

Hitherto we have been considering in outline the treatment of goods or services bought and sold. What of another class or business, intellectual property. What exactly is it, what are some of its characteristics, and how does it impinge upon the contracts function?

A pause to consider all this is indeed appropriate. The term 'intellectual property' is of fairly recent origin and is not generally defined. Developed from an earlier term 'industrial property' it is now normally held to include patent rights, trade marks, copyright, registered designs, design rights (in the UK) and (though not strictly intellectual property) trade secrets, which can include information given and received in confidence. Ancillary is the right to prevent others from 'passing off' their goods or services as our own, and in USA 'trade dress' where, for instance, a small chain of burger bars imitates the appearance of another better known one, so as to incline the public to assume the two are in association.

Notably, intellectual property now explicitly includes proprietary computer software, which can be protected by copyright and, under certain circumstances, by patent. Thus there are few businesses today which are unaffected. Penalties for casual infringement of rights can be severe enough, but systematic intentional infringement can, if discovered, lead to summary searches and the impounding of key company documents while legal proceedings are being instituted.

The main and usual interaction between intellectual property rights and contract work tends to be in the terms and conditions of certain agreements. Agreements for the purchase of computer hardware, for instance, will usually contain within them clauses licensing the user to use (which means copy) protected programs that are supplied by the manufacturer, who usually warrants that he possesses those rights. More elaborate terms and conditions will be provided by software suppliers, and in each case there are likely to be stringent restrictions upon use outside the licensed organisation or elsewhere than upon the supplied equipment, save perhaps for backup purposes or in the event of machine failure.

A key feature in intellectual property, as against goods or services, is that it tends to be exploited commercially by the grant of licences or sub-licences rather than outright sale. Hence it is in some respects akin to real property. The owner of the right can be likened to the freeholder of a building, and various levels of licensee or sub-licensee compared to a hierarchy of lessees, sub-lessees and under-lessees, each perhaps having sole or shared rights over the whole or a part of the total property, with or without access to common parts or sub-routines. It may be dangerous to press such analogies too far however. What the contacts executive needs to know is:

- Are we the proprietors or 'freeholders' of some copyright or patented material?
- Are we in the business of granting rights to our customers, as 'tenants' so to speak?
- Are any of those rights exclusive, for instance, and if so are there processes to prevent us accidentally granting 'exclusives' on the same property to more than one licensee at the same time?
- Are we licensees or 'tenants' of other people's intellectual property, possibly with the right to use and to license our own customers to use?
- If so, are there processes to ensure that we abide by the conditions of our licence, pay due commissions or royalties when they fall due, and generally behave like good tenants-in-chief; so that we never get evicted, as it were, along with our licensee customers who will then promptly sue us for wrongful eviction from the rights which we have granted them, prior to taking all their future business elsewhere?

Real property

Next let us turn to real property – land, building, office accommodation – and consider whether this falls within our remit. If we are company secretaries we shall know a certain amount about our real property already. Many leases and contracts for sale, and all conveyances and mortgages will have been under seal, and will have been brought to us for attention. (If we have abolished the use of the seal we may have to ask ourselves what mechanisms exist for ensuring that documents issued as deeds are brought to the board's attention and ratified, but arguably that is not a prime concern of this book).

Real estate being a fairly technical branch of law, we shall probably have an external law firm handling most of this for us. If not, and unless we have relevant conveyancing experience within the organisation, we shall need to appoint such a firm at once.

If there are branches in Scotland a Scottish law firm will also be needed; likewise for Northern Ireland, the Irish Republic, and any other jurisdictions in which we may have property interests.

Law, however, is only one aspect of real estate. A reputable firm of surveyors and estate agents should always be available to us, with practical knowledge of the districts in which we operate.

The property market is specialised. Leases tend to be issued for very long periods of time, spanning more than one economic cycle. Consequently, commercial property developers and dealers think like chess players, planning many moves ahead. Leases often contain onerous obligations, some of which may survive vacation of the premises by many years. Sureties and guarantees are commonplace. Do we have access to the right expertise to handle all these issues?

- Do our surveyors and real estate lawyers know sufficient about our business plans to be able to advise us sensibly? Do we indeed have long-term business plans with property in mind? To the extent that we do not, our actions will be influenced by short-term considerations and we shall be to an extent at the mercy of temporary market forces.
- Do we have adequate internal arrangements to ensure that our premises are being administered by someone who knows the terms of our occupation?
- Are the landlord and tenant obligations being observed?
- Do we seek any appropriate landlords' licenses when we make internal changes?
- Is the fire officer informed? And the fire prevention officer? And the insurance brokers?

It may not be necessary for a building administrator to have detailed knowledge in all of these areas. Access to the knowledge, and a good common-sense approach which knows when to seek it can be essential. In contractual terms, are there files on all these matters? Is there a periodic document muster, with the aid of the conveyancing lawyers, to confirm that all original documents are accounted for and complete? Because of the long time periods involved, and the relatively infrequent need to refer to some of this material, losses of key deeds and other records can pass unnoticed for many years.

Contracts with people

Since a company is not a natural person in law, virtually all of its acts are done on its behalf by human agents. These can fall into various categories: directors and officers, employees, and other agents or contractors.

Directors, especially non-executives, are likely to have contracts with the company in their capacity as members of the board. They may also have contracts of service as employees, though this is not essential.

Employment law, and particularly employment protection legislation, is intricate and today needs specialist treatment. Do we have a personnel or human resources unit qualified to handle these matters, and do they have adequate records of employees' contracts of service?

According to the circumstances we may not need to concern ourselves deeply with such matters. However, we should know whether there are standard contracts of service and whether they contain adequate clauses to protect confidentiality and intellectual property both during employment and after a staff member leaves.

Consultants and other specialists

Let us now turn to contracts for the supply of consultants and other specialists who may work for us as independent contractors. Are there written agreements for each of these, and who has them? Are they dealt with under the standard procurement routines that we may have, or do Personnel handle them, or are they 'anybody's baby'? If there is an appreciable number of these people it may be important to bring them within a suitable form of control. Key issues may be:

- Who decides that they are needed, and how?
- Are they providing skills not otherwise available, or are they there to augment resources at peak times?
- Who negotiates (and checks out) their fee rates?
- Are there suitable clauses dealing with the substitution of key people?
- Have we adequately covered the personal income tax situation, such that tax is being withheld unless appropriate Inland Revenue clearance demonstrated?
- And if any of these people are providing professional or fiduciary services which could leave us exposed, do we require suitable professional indemnity insurance or bonding? Or even 'key man' insurance?
- Some of these contractors may provide maintenance or 'help desk' services. Does anyone review the frequency of use and 'helpfulness' of the services?

- Finally do we provide any such services to our own customers or clients, and is that being managed through our sales processes?

Other areas of concern

Are there other contractual areas that we may have overlooked? Do we provide warranties or indemnities to third parties, and for how long? Are there any which survive termination of contracts, but which at some time in the future – when they might be long forgotten – might give rise to substantial claims?

If we are in this kind of business, let us consider how far we can reduce our exposure by insurance. Business is inherently risky. The key is to devise methods of controlling or managing the risk.

Taking control

Having surveyed the situation, we are now in a better position to comment upon any terms of reference that may have been given us, and possibly to write our own. Once again the approach we take will be peculiar to us and to our organisation. There are no textbook solutions which can be relied upon, but here are some key questions to help us.

Looking for the risk areas

Where are the principal contractual risks as we perceive them? We might define a 'principal risk' thus:

A principal risk is a situation which, if unchecked, could threaten the organisation as a whole.

These situations must be attended to first. They might include highly speculative fixed price contracts in areas with which we are unfamiliar, or deals in which unlikely but heavy penalties could be incurred for failure, delay or negligence. They might include other aspects special to our business which have critical factors in them. Once we know what they are, they become 'board business' right away, and under 'Cadbury' rules we probably have a duty to report them to the board at once.

The Cadbury rules stem from the Cadbury Code of Best Practice, which is now mandatory for companies listed on the Stock Exchange, and persuasive for many other organisations. Under item 1.4 of the Code there is a duty to keep the board of directors informed of significant matters, to ensure that the board is properly in control of the company.

Then let us look at secondary levels of risk. These we may define as contractual matters which, whilst not in themselves critical to the organisation, nonetheless represent a degree of exposure which justify special attention. They should be examined by those who do not benefit from their promotion. They may include specialist business areas which would benefit from multi-disciplinary review before contracts are cleared, or even standard relatively low-risk deals where the sheer size or value is such as to warrant attention. Financial and possibly legal specialists should be involved, in addition to whatever usual sales, costing and estimating procedures may be observed. To the extent that that may be deemed 'material', they are board business under Cadbury and should be reviewed either by the board or a board-appointed committee.

At a lower level of risk there may be much routine business where any risks are diversified over wide customer or product bases, so that a relative disaster in one situation would statistically be insignificant when taken together with that market as a whole. These we may feel should be controlled as a matter of 'best practice', rather than because in themselves they may be threatening.

Such considerations will influence where we direct our initial thrust.

Levels of involvement

Some questions need to be settled without delay: are we merely to administer contracts matters or do we take control, and in which respects? Where does our involvement start and finish?

This may be a matter of organisational need and also of the culture of the enterprise. For instance, in an organisation where contracts or jobs are managed by people chosen for their abilities in technical management, and where it is felt wasteful to concern such people with matters of commercial awareness, a very high degree of contracts support may be needed in every stage of the process. Not only must we take a leading part in the contracts negotiations, but we may also have to field a player at most of the progress meetings, and certainly whenever variation or change orders are being proposed and priced. We may even have to oversee the costing and execution procedures, so as to recognise when stages have been reached in the contract where payments on account may be demanded, and so as to be able to calculate and demand these sums. In this situation we might even need as many contracts staff as there are current contracts, or even more.

At the other end of the spectrum, our sales, production and technical people may have a high commercial awareness and level of experience, with profit responsibility and the authority to take many business and commercial decisions themselves. In such cases a contracts unit might be given the task of offering advice and support, with the onus of interpretation and implementation placed squarely upon the line management. In such a case our own terms of reference can be less burdensome and the staffing levels allowed us correspondingly lower.

Having established the degree of involvement which is necessary and acceptable, let us turn to some 'tools of the trade' which can help us keep account of what is going on and ensure that our intervention is positive and timely.

Designing a contracts register for control

We have already discussed the need for an early warning system, based upon sales reporting. We shall now need a contracts register. In an ideal world, the two may be combined. Let us consider some of the items of information or 'data fields' which we might expect to record in a relatively simple system:

Item or bid number: This might be a number ascribed by the Sales Department whenever a prospect becomes serious, or it might be the tender or bid reference.

Customer or prospect name: This might be an abbreviated version, but should be uniquely identifiable.

Entry date: There might be several dates to record. This might be the date upon which authority was given to spend time and money on the bid.

Name of project: This might be a mnemonic, or even a reference number ascribed by the prospective customer.

Salesman or bid manager: This is an important item. If the prospective sale becomes a 'win' we need a name to chase in order to establish that a contract is being agreed.

Project manager, if different: We shall certainly need him too.

Win or loss state: If blank, the outcome is still uncertain. Losses we can forget. Wins must be highlighted and pursued . . .

Start date: . . . and pursued urgently if the work is about to start.

Contract type: This might indicate the kind of contract (time and materials, fixed price, copyright licence) or it might be developed to indicate the risk level to assist us in placing maximum effort where it is needed.

End date: This indicates how long the contract is to run.

Value: This provides another indication of the size and (to an extent) of potential risk.

Special terms: Features like 'time the essence' if they matter to us, or a high exposure to consequential loss.

Job or project reference: In a perfect world *we* get to control the issue of these; and we only issue them after we are happy that contractual cover exists. If this authority is not available to us for whatever reason, we may have to decline responsibility for any work which gets started without a contract and for which payment becomes hard to collect.

An example of how such a contracts register might look is given in Figure 1. Figure 2, action report: wins in start date order, shows how by a simple reordering of the spreadsheet a useful summary can be produced for chasing purposes.

Bid No	Prospect	Date	Project	Bid Mgr.	Project Mgr.	Win/Loss	Start Date	Type	End Date	Value £K	Special/Comments	Job No/Contract Ref
1	Railtrak	2.1.96	Track Revue	FJW	kj	W	1.4.96	FP	31.3.97	100	Time the Essence	1234
2	Brit Aerosp	8.1.96	Autopilot	FJW	br	L	15.5.96					
3	Unilever	8.1.96	Soap Mfg.	KFR	qff	L	1.3.96					
4	BP	10.1.96	Pipelines	CBM	tr	W	1.4.96		31.12.96	50	Letter of Instr.	
5	MOD	10.1.96	K1234/96	CBT	prm	W	1.6.96	GC/STORES/1	31.5.97	150	L. of L.	
6	Glaxo	12.1.96	Inventory	CBF	tra	L	1.4.96					
7	Railtrak	12.1.96	Track 2	KR	pb		1.7.96					
8	Symonds Engr	31.1.96	Inventory	CBF	cw	L	1.3.96					
9	Baillie	31.1.96	Warehouse	CBF	pb	L	1.3.96					
10	Hill & Smith	31.1.96	Raw Mtl.	TTF	kj?	W	1.4.96	T + M	?	negotiable	Awaiting their lawyer	
11	Shell	31.1.96	Refinery S.	CBM	pb?	W	1.9.96	FP	31.12.97	500	Inst Purch & Supply	
12	Brit Gas	1.2.96.	Gas Gather	CBM	tra?	W	1.9.96	?				
13	BAT	1.3.96	B&W	HBR			1.10.96					
14	Vauxhall	1.3.96	Vehicle CKD	FJW			1.10.96					
15	Ford	1.4.96	Inventory2	CBF			1.10.96					
16	Nissan	1.4.96	Quality Review	MR			?					
17												
18												
19												
20												
21												
22												
23												
24												
25												
26												
27												
28												

Figure 1 Combined win/loss contracts register.

Bid No	Prospect	Date	Project	Bid Mgr.	Project Mgr.	Win/Loss	Start Date	Type	End Date	Value £K	Special/Comments	Job No/Contract Ref
1	Railtrak	2.1.96	Track Revue	FJW	kj	W	1.4.96	FP	31.3.97	100	Time the Essence	1234
4	BP	10.1.96	Pipelines	CBM	tr	W	1.4.96		31.12.96	50	Letter of Instr.	
10	Hill & Smith	31.1.96	Raw Mtl.	TTF	kj?	W	1.4.96	T + M	?	negotiable	Awaiting their lawyer	
5	MOD	10.1.96	K1234/96	CBT	prm	W	1.6.96	GC/STORES/1	31.5.97	150	L. of L.	
11	Shell	31.1.96	Refinery S.	CBM	pb?	W	1.9.96	FP	31.12.97	500	Inst Purch & Supply	
12	Brit Gas	1.2.96.	Gas Gather	CBM	tra?	W	1.9.96	?				

Figure 2 Action report: wins in start date order.

Contract clearance

In a copy book situation, proper negotiations will have taken place, either before a bid is won, or between the time of closing the sale and the time a job is due to start. A contract may have been proposed by one side or the other, debated over, and finally signed. This enables a formal clearance procedure to be observed. If we have control or influence over the release of the work order, we can exercise control in a logical sequence. But let us now look at a few of the things that can go wrong, to frustrate us in this process.

Dealing with emergencies

Prominent among these is the 'crash programme that cannot wait'. For one reason or another our sales people have closed a deal rapidly with the clear understanding that, because of the urgency, work must start on Monday next. 'No time for contracts, lawyers and all that stuff', we are told. 'Give us a job number, quick'.

A practical hint: If the situation is simple, issue not only a job number but also a standard sales order complete with standard terms and conditions, and send it to the customer at once.

Not all situations are simple. We need a prepared response, and here is one. There may be nothing to prevent even a long-term, fixed price, risky job starting rapidly without a contract *provided we obtain legally binding temporary cover for it*. Beware of 'letters of intent'. Notice that our customer *intends* to place a contract may not help us, unless we are offering a standard, production line item that can easily be reassigned if and when the intent wavers, as it is legally liable to do. Try soliciting a letter such as the one on the following page.

Although there may be a little debate over words like 'irrevocable', and you might be asked to accept a limit of liability, these matters are amenable to agreement over the telephone, confirmed by email or fax (in these days of rapid communication) and subsequently confirmed by 'hard copy' correspondence if matters really are urgent. Beware of accepting statements that there is no time for such formalities, or that no one on the other side has authority to comply. If matters really are urgent, if our stance is a reasonable one, and if we stand firm, it can be surprising how rules get re-interpreted.

'The one that got away'

Let us now consider an instance where matters have gone further. Our control procedures didn't work. Someone has jumped the gun. A job has been in process for some while without contractual cover. A good deal of work has been done.

ABC Engineering Limited
Unit 500
Slough Trading Estate
Slough

To the Contracts Manager
DEF Communications Limited
Blackfriars
London EC2

Dear Sir,

XYZ Project – Your Tender No 96/1848

You are hereby authorised to commence work without delay upon the XYZ Project as previously discussed between us, on the basis that until the matter has proceeded to formal contract we irrevocably undertake to pay for all staff time expended by you at your current standard rates plus materials and other disbursements, billable by you monthly and settled by us within 30 days. The contract price, when negotiated, will be adjusted to reflect this instruction.

Yours faithfully,

For and On behalf of ABC Engineering Limited
A B Smith
Company Secretary.

Nothing is in writing yet, and such contract drafts as exist refer to a stage payment due 'upon signature' which, for one reason or another, is clearly not going to happen in a hurry. Yet we need that payment.

Here it may help to recall that under the Law of England, *a simple contract may be implied by conduct.* The term 'simple' is a technicality and does not refer to size or complexity. Provided that we can establish with reasonable certainty what we and the customer intended at the outset, and provided the conduct of both sides has been consistent with an agreement being in force, we can probably press for that payment, if necessary suing and claiming partial performance. Prevarication on the part of the other side's negotiators to delay negotiation on the 'small print' and final signature need not be allowed to cause us financial loss.

All this is of course highly undesirable. Prevention is far better than cure.

Other techniques

What other devices are available to us in establishing contracts supervision or control? Here are a few to be thinking about:

- Developing a contracts clearance routine with standard company paperwork.
- Introducing a risk analysis system, using feedback from known past 'failures'.
- Enlisting our colleagues' support – the 'contracts road show'.
- Targeting recently appointed managers.
- Influencing how projects are run:
  project logs
  everything in writing
  the time and materials philosophy
  the fixed price philosophy
  variation or change orders
- Devising 'plain men's guides' to difficult documents.
- Establishing an authorities procedure; an example is shown in Figure 3.

Seek to get the balance right

Most well managed organisations produce authority level documents such as the one shown in Figure 3, and most managements affirm that they could not keep proper control without them. They are probably right; indeed, many such documents are much longer than the one given, and they refer to many more procedures and forms to be filled in order to get approvals.

Now stop and read Chapter 7, 'Techniques of negotiating'. There you will see that the toughest deadlines and other constraints that are put upon us when we are negotiating with customers and suppliers are the ones put upon us by our own organisation. Yet we are both supposed to be on the same side!

Strive to ensure that organisational controls are adequate to protect us against the 'runaway horses' in our organisation, and yet flexible enough to serve the winners of good business. The board may indeed only meet once a month, and they will not appreciate unnecessary 'panic' requests for clearances between meetings. Yet happy is the organisation that recognises the exceptional 'main chance' when it occurs, and wise is the company secretary who knows where his directors can be telephoned for approval if the need arises!

Summary

Surveying the scene

1. Find out who has control over relationships with customers, suppliers, staff, landlords, tenants, and users of intellectual property (ours and other people's). Go on a company 'walkabout'.

Category	Item	Level 1	Level 2	Level 3	Board	Functional Authority Involvement:				
						Human Resources	Production Engineering/ Mfg	Office Services	Sales	Purchasing
Capital Expenditure	All Items	£ -	£ 5,000.00	£ 10,000.00	Above			As Appropriate		
Revenue Expenditure	Raw Mtls	£ 500.00	£ 10,000.00	£ 50,000.00	Above		Yes			
	Components	£ 250.00	£ 5,000.00	£ 25,000.00	Above		Yes			
	Tooling	£ -	£ -	£ 10,000.00	Above		Yes			
	Company Vehicles	£ -	£ -	£ 20,000.00	Above	Yes	Works Vehicles Only			
	New Staff (Salary Levels)	£ -	£ 15,000.00	£ 25,000.00	Above	Yes				
	Wage/Salary Reviews	Grade 1	Grades 2-5	Grades 5-9	Above	Yes				
Other	Disciplinary	Verbal Warnings	Written Warnings	Dismissals	Senior Dismissals	Yes				
Sales Contracts	Risk Categories	A	B-C	D	Above		Yes		Yes	Yes

All items not covered above to be submitted to the Company Secretary for Board Clearance as necessary. Time should be allowed for this.

Deeds require clearance by the Company Secretary and one director - normally the functional director concerned. Time needs to be allowed for this. The submitting department is responsible for briefing the appropriate Board Member.

Level 1 comprises Section Managers
Level 2 comprises Division Managers
Level 3 comprises Executive Directors

The Board meets monthly, and submissions must reach the Company Secretary no later than 25th day of the month preceding.

Figure 3 Example of an authority level schedule.

2. Analyse where the main risks lie. How is authority delegated and applied to manage them?
3. Seek access to 'early warning' information.
4. Focus first upon areas where the least effort will produce the greatest enhancement of control.
5. Ensure that the contracts function's terms of reference pass the PRAMKU test.
6. Take time before finalising those terms of reference. Allow for revisions in the light of experience.
7. Make certain your own lines of responsibility are clear.

Taking control

8. Define 'material risks'. Check that we are compliant with the Cadbury code in handling them.
9. Examine secondary but significant risks.
10. Establish a realistic/necessary level of involvement in contracts activities.
11. Design and implement a contract register system which gives effective control.
12. Introduce a contract clearance routine which involves the right people with the right skills to understand what they are letting the company in for.
13. Devise 'safety valve' procedures for 'the job that cannot wait'. Strive to get the overall balance right.

2
Knowing contract law

The first point to be made about contract law, as with most other branches of knowledge, is that it can be as important to know where to go to find things out as to have the knowledge fully memorised in one's head. We do, however, need a sufficient grasp of the law to facilitate such 'knee jerk reactions' as may be necessary in everyday business life and to sense when further study is needed. A sufficient grasp of essentials is, perhaps, the most that a book of this kind can expect to provide.

What is a contract?

The law of contract is a part of mercantile law which has been developed over the centuries as merchants have done business with each other. Of all branches of English law it is one of the most stable because it is based substantially upon common rather than statute law. Unlike the Companies Acts, which contain many arbitrary tenets and rules of recent origin which are likely to be changed considerably from time to time as Parliament decides, contract law stays much the same from one decade to the next. Because of this, and because judges have been able (in common law countries at least) to try whenever possible to give effect to the intention of the parties rather than have regard only to the form in which it may have been expressed, it is possible with a little experience to get a 'feel' for what the law is. This makes it worthwhile for us to take the time to study it in some depth, both the theory and the practice.

What then is a contract? It is an agreement between two or more parties which confers *personal* rights and imposes *personal* obligations upon the parties to it. It should be distinguished from other types of agreement or undertaking which may have to do with rights and obligations in *things*. Conveyances in land are examples of these.

The personal nature of a contract, however, does not mean that it is in any sense a lesser part of the law of the land. A breach of contract is just as illegal as trespass, non-payment of rates and taxes, libel, slander, negligence or any other tort (which is a breach of civil law), and failure to pay one's taxes in time, which is a breach of statute law. Since contract law is founded in common law, it may be worthwhile to summarise the three main aspects of law in common law countries such as England.

Common law: These are the rules developed over the centuries by judges to determine, upon as consistent a basis as possible 'what the law is' in any given set of circumstances. Originally common law remedies were only obtainable in the King's or Queen's Bench, under the Lord Chief Justice.

Equity: Equity comprises supplementary rules of 'fair play' developed to mitigate or modify some of the harsher and more rigid effects of common law. Originally this was administered only in the Court of Chancery, presided over by the Lord Chancellor as 'Keeper of the King's Conscience'. Until the second half of the nineteenth century, equity was administered quite separately from common law so that a litigant might find himself suing twice to obtain the right measure of justice.

Statute law: The making of laws by Act of Parliament.

Case law: The system, which applies to common law, equity and statute law alike, of establishing precedents in each specific lawsuit, which then influence all subsequent situations of the same or a similar kind. They tend to be binding upon courts of lesser status, and persuasive upon courts of the same ranking. Superior courts may, if they so decide, supplant junior case law with overriding decisions of their own, which then in turn become the definitive decisions.

Statute law overrides all the other forms of law, though the interpretation of it will be decided through case law. In general, the courts will have regard to the written word of the Act and not to the arguments in Parliament which led to the framing of it, although there has recently been some movement in the interpretation of this principle.

Equity normally overrides common law where the two may conflict, although judges will order a common law remedy in preference to an equitable one if they consider that it offers the plaintiff adequate redress. There are certain prerequisites, known as the 'equitable principles', however, which may inhibit someone from obtaining the kind of court action in equity which they might prefer. Two of these are 'he who comes to the court seeking equity must come with clean hands', and 'equity considers that to have been done which ought to have been done'. Framed in late mediaeval times, these principles nonetheless can have a dramatic effect upon twentieth-century legal remedies, as we shall see.

In very early times there was no contract law as such, and legal redress could only be had for well defined acts in the rural society of those days, such as trespass, non-payment of rent, or breach of covenant. All these were the common law causes of action. As mercantile activity developed, so did the need to enforce commercial undertakings, so that contract law of today encompasses or is influenced by all of the branches, common law, equity and statute law (notably the Sale of Goods Act, the Unfair Contracts Terms Act and the consumer protection laws of the past few decades).

Summary

1. Contract law is concerned with *personal* rights and obligations between those who agree to be bound to one another.

2. It is just as binding *upon those parties* as any other parts of the law.
3. *What the parties meant* is important.

Kinds of contract

There are three basic kinds of contract: a contract by deed, a contract of record, and a simple contract.

The first of these is a *contract by deed*, or a *contract under seal*. The key elements of a deed are:

1. That it shall be *in writing*.
2. That it shall be *sealed* (no longer a legal requirement where it is 'signed as a deed'). In ancient times this meant what it said, since most of the population could not write. Today, legal practitioners affix a wafer representing the seal upon which, strictly speaking, the party should place his finger before witnesses.
3. That it shall be *signed by the promisor*. If the party is not a natural person, the corporate seal will be affixed instead and it will be witnessed in accordance with the Articles or other constitution. If the corporation has elected to dispense with the seal, and its Articles amended, one can rely upon a written statement that it is being issued 'as a deed' and witnessed, normally by two directors or one director and the secretary. Signatures of individuals are normally witnessed also, and this would cover for the fairly rare instance of someone being unable to write.
4. That it shall be *'delivered'*, unless the party in question is a corporation. At one time delivery was evidenced by the promisor declaring 'I deliver this as my Act and Deed' before the witnesses. In these less formal times delivery may be implied by conduct or may be achieved by posting the document to the counterparty. A more legal definition of 'delivery' might be the final and absolute transfer of the deed, properly executed, in such a manner that it becomes irrevocable. The intention of the promisor can be a key factor, and on occasion delivery can be implied by conduct.

Why all the formality, one might ask? The key feature of a deed is that it is a more solemn undertaking than other kinds of contract. Essential for certain purposes such as the transfer of interests in land, a deed is encountered also in day-to-day commercial contracts where one of the parties is a local authority or public utility. Such bodies can sometimes only give valid undertakings under seal. In the case of a trading company, it is one way of helping to ensure that whoever entered into the contract was empowered to do so. The seal being normally the instrument of the directors, it is harder for the board to avoid responsibility for its use. There does not have to be a counterparty to a deed, but where there is one, he must *assent* to it for the document to be valid. This might be done by drafting him into the document so that he, too, signs seals and delivers a copy. In addition, legal actions can be brought for a period of 12 years. Normally this period is six years for undertakings not by deed. There does not have to be 'consideration' for the transaction, or value given.

Under the 1989 Companies Act a company does not have to use a seal. If it has elected not to do so (and altered its Articles if necessary) it can execute a deed if it is signed by two directors, or by one director and the company secretary. If the seal is not affixed, there needs to be some wording to indicate its status, such as '. . . Signed as a Deed, for and on behalf of XYZ Limited.' Where solicitors are involved, they should be told that a seal is not in use. As previously stated, an individual can sign a document 'as a deed' without sealing it.

Frequently a deed will be professionally drafted.

Summary

1. A deed must be in writing.
2. It may be sealed.
3. It is signed and witnessed by the person who is promising.
4. It must be 'delivered'.

Another form of contract is a *contract of record*. This kind of contract is imposed by a court as a result of legal proceedings, and is not properly the concern of this book.

A simple contract

The third and most significant kind of contract from our viewpoint is the *simple contract*. This is today the basis for most commercial activity because of its convenience and versatility. The essential elements of a simple contract are as follows:

1. There must be *agreement* between the parties at the time they make the contract.
2. The terms must be *reasonably clear*.
3. There must have been an *intention to create a legal relationship*.
4. There must be *consideration*, or *value given*. This is not necessary under the Law of Scotland, nor in England if a deed is executed.

Agreement may be expressed or implied. If it is expressed, then one way of demonstrating it is by the process of *offer and acceptance*. There are certain rules which have to be observed if offer and acceptance is to be valid.

Offer and acceptance

An offer, to be valid, must be capable of giving rise to a legally binding agreement there and then. An Invitation to Tender, for instance, is not an offer. It is merely an invitation to make an offer or to engage in some other kind of communication from which business might arise. It might indicate that, to merit consideration by the buyer, any tender we make must be in the form of an offer. We may be asked to undertake to keep our offer open for a given length of time, and we may be required to submit some kind of surety such as a bid bond, to protect the buyer from the cost of examining our proposals only to have us withdraw at the last minute. But that in itself does not make the Invitation to Tender an offer.

A sales proposal, on the other hand, may or may not be a legally binding offer according to the way we word it. This is why many organisations insert the words 'subject to contract' in their proposal documentation. It allows time and an opportunity for later discussion upon detail before anyone is irrevocably committed.

A standard price list is not an offer. It is an indication of the terms under which business may be done if the buyer makes an offer and if that offer is accepted. Similarly, priced goods in a shop window or a showroom do not themselves constitute offers, though there is legislation now to prevent what is considered abuse, especially as regards private buyers or consumers. A public advertisement may or may not be an offer according to the wording. Note that most mail order operations require a form to be filled by the intending purchaser, often with space for a credit card number. That is where the offer starts, for reasons which will be obvious.

An offer must be made by the offeror, brought to the knowledge of the offeree, and accepted – in that order – for a contract to have been formed. Acceptance in those circumstances has to be unconditional. If the offeree tries to accept with conditions attached, or with variations, then he makes what is regarded as a counter-offer. A counter-offer 'kills' the original offer, so that the first offeror is no longer bound by it, and it constitutes a further offer. This does not prevent the offeree enquiring further about the terms, provided it is clear that this is what is happening.

An offeree can be an individual, or an unnatural person such as a company. It can be a class of people, such as 'all the ordinary shareholders in the XYZ Corporation'. It can be the public at large, such as the potential customers of a news vendor.

Summary

1. An offer has to be capable of becoming binding when it is made. A mere invitation will not do.
2. A price list on its own is not an offer. Nor (usually) is an advertisement.
3. A valid offer must be (a) made, (b) brought to the knowledge of the other party or parties, and (c) accepted – in that order – to be valid.
4. The acceptance must be unconditional and in the form required.
5. Once it has been properly made there is 'agreement'. That is what makes the contract.

Offers, counter-offers and lapses

Now let us consider the offer a little further. It can be accepted unconditionally, in which case it immediately becomes a contract. It can be extinguished and supplanted by a *counter-offer*. It can be *rejected outright*, in which case it ceases at once. The offeror is thus released, even though the offeree almost immediately changes his mind and seeks to reinstate it. It can be *revoked*. And it can *lapse*.

Changes of mind

How does an offer get *revoked*? To release himself from an offer upon which he has changed his mind, the offeror must communicate his change of mind to the offeree. Revocation may be implied by the conduct of the offeror, but awareness of that conduct must reach the offeror before a revocation becomes valid. If by that time the offeree has already indicated acceptance, either to the offeror or to a duly appointed agent of that offeror, then a contract will result and the offeror will be bound by it.

Acceptance in these circumstances will be valid if it complies with the requirements of the offer, if there are any, such as 'by first class registered post' or 'by fax' or 'by email' even. If no procedures for valid acceptance are stated, then it will be presumed that the acceptor may use the same means as the offeror used in making his offer. Verbal methods such as telephone or word of mouth are quite legal. The problem here can be in proving just what happened and when, which is why stringent independent methods of written confirmation and audit are used by banks engaged in foreign exchange dealing, where much business can be done verbally for substantial amounts.

More about lapses

How and when does an offer lapse? An offer may lapse if either party dies. It may lapse after the expiry of a time limit stated in the offer, or if no time was stated, then after a 'reasonable time', however that may be decided. It may lapse if it was made on a contingency, once that contingency no longer exists. So an offer by Company A to carry out a work package for Company B at a certain price provided that Company B wins a hoped for contract with Overseas Government C, will lapse as soon as that government has awarded the contract to someone else. A word of warning, however: Just because a supplier states in his offer that 'it will be valid for 90 days' or 'until the Overseas Government decision is known', there is nothing to prevent him from revoking it in the meantime. If we wish to hold him to it for a period, we either have to make a full contract with him, with a conditional clause in it, or agree a separate option agreement for a fee. Some business is tendered ignoring this principle because of the presumption that no sub-contractor will risk upsetting a tender process in this way. However, it is not legally sound.

More about acceptance

Let us now look a little more closely at the process of acceptance. It has to be in the manner required or allowed for in the terms of the offer, or it can be in the manner of its presentation. It also has to be communicated to the offeror or his agent. Alternatively, and if this is not inconsistent with the terms of the offer, acceptance can be implied by the offeree's conduct if that is clear and unambiguous. In certain contractual situations where legal processes are slow and work may have started for sound practical reasons with the full knowledge and acquiescence of both sides, this can be a useful tool for the contracts manager.

Problems with the Post Office

The post as the sole means of communication is becoming less common in contract work, which is possibly just as well in view of a curious legal precedent known as the Postal Rule. This holds that when the post is considered a normal means of communication in the business, and where it has been employed by the offeror, the Post Office is deemed to be the offeror's appointed agent. So that a revocation reaching the offeree at any time after he has posted his reply is invalid. It is invalid if delays cause that acceptance letter to arrive three weeks later, or even if it gets lost in the post and never arrives. All the offeree has to do is provide evidence and time of posting. Operations involving significant use of the postal services in circumstances where this rule could cause problems normally word the 'small print' of their offers so as to exclude it.

Certainty of meaning

A contract, to be valid, must be sufficiently certain that 'a reasonable man conversant with the circumstances' can understand with sufficient clarity what was intended. Since in the final analysis a judge will decide such matters, this means that a contracts officer needs to ask himself this question:

'What might a judge consider that "the man on the Clapham omnibus" – properly briefed – would think that the parties meant at the time they made the contract?'

This is quite a tall order! To the extent that the judge feels he can answer this question with confidence, he may be assured that there is a contract. To the extent that he may be unsure, there is a risk that the judge would strike out completely the parts of the agreement which failed the test. If those parts struck at *the essence of the agreement itself* – the manner in which the price was to be arrived at, for instance – then the whole contract might be declared void. Time taken in making contracts clear and unambiguous is always time well spent. Simple language and short sentences are quite permissible.

It is sometimes possible to cite a rule known as *quantum meruit*, which provides that the supplier gets 'as much as he deserves' for work done. The processes for establishing a figure under *quantum meruit* can be quite arbitrary, however, and might well not yield the full profit which would otherwise apply.

Making it legal

To make a legal contract both parties must intend it to be legally binding. A voluntary undertaking does not of itself become a contract, and the only way under English law to make it binding is to execute it under seal, as with a deed of gift, a charitable covenant or – in the case of an individual – a deed poll.

There is always a risk, however, that documents in the later stages of drafting can begin to look like contracts. That is why many companies place the words 'subject to contract' upon every version except the last.

Particular care needs to be taken in handling documents entitled '*heads of agreement*' which on occasion can appear very formal indeed. The term has no precise meaning save that which may be ascribed to it in the body of the text itself.

Sometimes it is meant to be merely a summary of the principal areas of consent which, other things being equal, will be included in a formal contract later if both parties still agree, with or without additional material which may occur to the parties after further thought. At other times there can be a mutual understanding that it virtually contains all the subject matter and will only be altered to include what is sometimes called 'boiler plate' – a battery of commonly used standard clauses.

Occasionally heads of agreement will contain very precise phraseology in certain areas and only outline clauses elsewhere. In such cases it might be assumed that those parts which are precisely framed will not be altered, whereas the other parts will. Quite often both parties reckon they know what they mean by it without having to spell it out. Sometimes they are right! Hence it is crucial that it is made clear on the face of the document whether or not the heads of agreement are legally binding.

Consideration or value

What then of *consideration*? The simplest form of consideration, because there can be little argument, is money, and most contracts are drafted to encompass a monetary value. There is no reason why goods or services should not be cited, but take care not to offer past services or supplies as consideration. That would not be valid, and the contract would not be properly formed.

Different ways of making a simple contract

It is probably in considering the possible forms that a simple contract may take that one fully appreciates the practicality and convenience of this branch of law. For a contract may be *in writing*, or *verbal*, or even *implied by conduct*. Statute law varies this to some extent, in that contracts for the sale of land and for certain other purposes must be in writing. Most commercial contracts are in fact written for the purpose of avoiding doubt and provision of evidence, but they do not need to be. In addition to foreign exchange deals, which we have already discussed, hotel bookings, theatre tickets, insertions in local newspapers are ordered and committed over the telephone. Payment by credit card is similarly dealt with, although in this case there is invariably some background 'small print' which governs their use.

When we board a bus there is an implied contract that the conductor will take us where we wish to go on the bus route, that we shall pay the stated fare, and that the whole contract will be governed by some small print which may be displayed somewhere in the bus garage, a copy of which we could obtain if we wished, but which neither we nor the conductor have troubled to examine that day. This principle can, with care, be extended where necessary into the commercial and industrial sphere. A contractor commences work on a customer's site. Over a period the needs of the job vary to some extent from that specified in the written agreement. Both parties know this, and both parties allow the contractor to vary his work on the presumption that what he is doing is fair and reasonable, that it meets the needs of the site, and that where it is possible to deduce the prices or rates for this divergent work, payment will be due. Unless there are clauses which specifically regulate it, those variations will become part of the contract as if they had been written. Even if there are clauses requiring such changes to be agreed in writing, if each party ignores them, then after a while the conduct will be deemed to override the form of the written agreement. Convenience has its dangers!

Some conditions in contracts are *implied by statute law*. Notable among these are the warranties of satisfactory quality and fitness for purpose under the Sale of Goods Act 1979. These, for instance, are always applicable when the buyer deals as a consumer or in his private capacity. They will be implied in other contracts for the sale of goods unless they are expressly excluded by agreement and that exclusion is reasonable.

Contracts that are flawed

What is apparently valid and enforceable under contract law can nonetheless be avoided in various ways. A contract may be *void*, which means that it has no effect in law upon either side. It can be *voidable*, meaning that the party which stands to lose from some inappropriate circumstance may elect whether to treat it as void or to stand by it, obliging the other party to honour his side of the bargain. A third category of frustration is that of *unenforceability*, which is a way of saying that although there is nothing wrong with the contract in law, it cannot be enforced owing to a technicality, possibly due to some evidence in writing not being available, as with a verbal contract to sell land.

Among void contracts are those where there has been genuine *mistake* as to the subject matter or the nature of the document itself. Other examples of genuine mistake are instances where each party believes the terms to be different. Where owing to mistaken information neither party would have agreed had they known the correct facts at the time, a court may regard the contract as unenforceable, but if it considers it capable of rectification the court may do so.

Other instances of void contracts are contracts to *commit crimes*, or *torts*, which are civil wrongs such as trespass, agreements *contrary to statute law*, contracts *in restraint of trade*, and to create restrictive practices or uphold resale price maintenance, as well as the rather vague area of being '*against the public interest*'. Prominent in commercial contract law is the issue of restraint of trade whereby a company may seek to prevent a former employee from setting up a business in opposition. Clauses in a contract of employment which seek to do this are harshly examined by the courts. The usual test is 'what is the least onerous interpretation against the employee which would afford the employer reasonable protection?'. If the offending clause cannot easily be amended by the judge because of the way it has been drafted, there is always the risk that it may be struck out altogether.

The whole area of restrictive practices is now a specialised area of law. Clauses may be void under the Restrictive Trade Practices Act 1976. If instances are significant enough and markets sufficiently substantial, European Union law may be brought to bear. Arrangements held to be restrictive may be void under Article 85(1) of the Treaty of Rome, under which fines of up to 10% of worldwide group turnover may also be imposed.

Ultra vires is an area with which we should be familiar. A company may not avoid its contracts to third parties merely by exceeding the powers given to it by its Articles of Association, but the same is not true as regards the implied contract it has with its members. That is to say the members can sue the directors if they consider they have suffered loss as a result of a contract which would have been void but for this protection of the counterparty.

Fulfilling contracts

How does a contract become fulfilled or discharged? It will be discharged when all those actions which were contracted to be done have been done by the parties concerned or at their behest. Where a contract is expressly for the performance by a named individual it is said to be a contract of service. In addition to employment contracts, agreements for specialists or consultants may come within this category. Unless otherwise agreed, such contracts can only be discharged by the individuals in person, and not by any alternative staff. Many firms of professional consultants and business advisers insert clauses in their contracts modifying this rule.

When time is important

When time is known to be crucial to one party at the time the contract was made, it is said to be 'of the essence' of the agreement. Hence supply of Christmas articles might be deemed to be required in time for the Christmas trade. Articles under sub-contract which are known to be necessary to meet a certain shipment date critical to the prime contract will fall within this definition. To supply them as much as one day late is regarded as a breach of contract which strikes at its very essence. The injured party in such a case may elect to accept the goods, or to reject them. In each case reparation may be obtained for any loss that has been suffered. To avoid any doubt, clauses are often inserted in contracts indicating a required delivery date and stating specifically that 'time shall be of the essence'. Yet it is not necessary to do this. If one party knew at the time the contract was made that time was of such importance, a 'time of the essence' clause can be implied.

Recognising 'time of the essence' situations is very important for every contracts administrator. If we are supplying standard articles which cannot be obtained from stock, and for which there might be a long manufacturing or supply time, we should be very wary of these situations.

The principle in breaches of 'time of the essence' situations can apply to other breaches of condition. 'Conditions' are fundamental to a contract. In each case the injured party may choose whether to require completion or to treat the contract as irrevocably broken. Damages may be obtained. Minor breaches of 'warranty' merely give a right to sue for damages.

Use of the 'condition precedent'

One feature of a contract which can be convenient, especially in setting up consortia of contractors and sub-contractors is the 'condition precedent'. A condition precedent is one that has to be satisfied before the contract becomes effective. It calls for the happening of some event or the performance of some act after the contract terms have been agreed on, before the contract shall be effective against the parties. Hence a group of sub-contractors might each offer cover to their prime contractor in the form of a fully binding contract, to enable him to tender to the end user or customer. Provided each sub-contract contains the clause 'It shall be a condition precedent to this agreement that the XYZ contract be awarded to Company A, the Prime Contractor', the mere fact of the award will then bring the contract into effect. The fact of its loss will automatically render all of the sub-contracts worthless without the need for further formality, which is frequently what everyone wants.

'Many contracts are burdensome: a few are "impossible"!'

It is important that the provisions for 'discharge under frustration' are understood. It cannot be emphasised too strongly that no one avoids a contract merely because it has become burdensome or unprofitable. It is not automatically void even if circumstances change and make it impossible, and the law here is complex. Among the 'boiler plate' clauses found in standard contract are those dealing with *force majeure*, circumstances beyond the control of the parties. It can be important to have these carefully drafted.

Under the provisions known as 'anticipatory breach of contract' if a party refuses to perform a key provision by either words or conduct, the result can be regarded as a breach of contract and can confer a right to sue. One such example is where relationships become strained and a customer refuses to make a stage payment where one is due, where there is no clause permitting him to do so.

Changing a contract

A contract, being a set of personal rights and obligations, can be altered at any time and in any way (provided it remains lawful) by agreement between the parties who set it up. There may even be the introduction of a third or more parties, one or more of whom may take over the liabilities of one of the original parties. The one constraint is that there must be agreement among the original signatories. In long-term contracts it is often necessary to vary the terms as the needs of the business change. This can very easily be achieved by the drafting of change or variation orders. If it is remembered that the rules of offer and acceptance apply, or of agreement by each party signing the same paper, little difficulty need arise.

Who are the participants?

Under a rule known as 'privity of contract', a person must be a party to a contract in order to enjoy its benefits or be bound by its obligations. It is particularly important to remember this in contracting and sub-contracting. Even when a sub-contractor is in close proximity to the ultimate client, working on his premises, interacting daily with him and his staff, if he fails in some respect to perform then the right of action is between the client and the prime contractor, and a separate action lies between the prime contractor and the party who is in breach. Unless there are specific arrangements linking the 'sub' to the client in some respect, the two parties have no legal relationship whatsoever. This rule has become prominent in recent years in the commercial property field. If an original long-term lease allows a tenant to sublet but not to assign, he can be liable to the landlord for the failure of future tenants for many years after he has physically vacated the premises.

Remedies when things go wrong

In predicting the likely outcome of breaches or threatened breaches of contract a general understanding of the difference between common law and equity becomes significant. There are three remedies for breach of contract.

The common law remedy

1. *Damages*, where the injured party becomes entitled to a sum of money to recompense for the financial loss suffered. The plaintiff may claim *fair compensation* for losses arising naturally from the breach. The accent is upon compensation for the plaintiff and *not punishment* for the defendant.

Moreover, from the time the plaintiff becomes aware of the breach or of the likelihood of the breach he becomes 'trustee in damages' for the defendant. This means that he has to start immediately to *mitigate or reduce his loss* in reasonable ways, and to look after the situation like a trustee might for the beneficiaries of a trust. In colloquial terms, the court will not allow him to 'take the defendant to the cleaners'. If he does so, the judge will calculate what lesser cost alternatives had been open to him, and will award any damages on the lesser sum.

There is a valuable lesson and an opportunity here for all contracts managers. When our organisation becomes aware that it may fail in performance, *it might be best to warn the other party at once.* Not only could this be good customer relations; it could actually save us money.

The equitable remedies

2. A *decree of specific performance.* In this case, the court issues a direction that the defendant shall perform the contract. Failure to do so may be regarded as *contempt of court,* leading to possible imprisonment by directors or officers.

3. An *injunction.* Injunctions are also *orders of the court,* and they can be of more than one kind. They might call upon one of the parties to cease and desist any breaches he may be committing. They may also attack any anticipatory breaches by requiring him not to commit any that are contemplated. Often they are granted quickly and sometimes *ex parte,* which means that the defendant was not involved at the time. In most cases injunctions are temporary, pending a full hearing of the case. It is common in *ex parte* proceedings for the plaintiff to be asked for financial guarantees or sureties in case he eventually loses his case, the defendant becomes entitled to damages owing to business interruption, and the plaintiff ultimately cannot pay.

Of these three kinds of remedy, the first is a common law redress and the other two are equitable. This means that *the court will always award damages in preference to the other two,* unless it considers that the plaintiff can only receive justice through an equitable remedy. And to obtain an equitable remedy the 'equitable doctrines' must have been observed, as regards fair and just behaviour.

This can mean that where one party to a contract has committed a significant and highly damaging breach and the other party has withheld a stage payment beyond the due date 'to try and get him to perform', if that withholding was itself the breach of another clause then the only remedy left to him might be in damages. He no longer 'comes to the court with clean hands', as it were.

Examples of 'specific performance' can occur in the domestic property market, in ways which may make the principle easy to understand. If I agree a price for an attractive estate designed house and the vendor fails to convey it, I shall be unlikely to obtain specific performance. The judge will advise me to find another similar house and to sue for my expenses and any difference in price. If, however, I have contracted for a 'stately home' which is of significance to me – perhaps because an illustrious ancestor of mine once owned it – then I may have a chance of convincing the court that nothing else will do me justice.

To take a commercial example, a computer systems house markets a hotel reservation and management system, for which an hotel modifies its reception area to accommodate special purpose hardware and software, and even buys the specific hardware itself. The systems house then finds it expedient to withdraw from the market, cuts its losses and tries to reach a financial settlement in *damages* with its customer. If there is no other comparable software package on the market which will do the job without further alteration to public areas of the hotel – and especially if the holiday period is about to begin – that systems house might be in danger of a decree of *specific performance*. Failure to perform could then put its directors in *contempt of court*.

Agreeing damages in advance

Because of the uncertainties of the law in adjudicating upon damages, and the problems of doing the arithmetic of 'mitigation' in practical circumstances, many commercial contracts contain 'liquidated damages' clauses. In simple terms, these clauses specify formulae for calculating damages in those circumstances which can be predicted. Common among these are 'liquidated damages for delay'. Typically, they will specify a few percentage points of the contract value for each week of delay, up to an agreed maximum, which will be payable to the injured party in lieu of what the actual damage was. Another version of the clause can specify liquidated damages in the event of total failure.

Misleading language

We have already discussed letters of intent and considered a draft of one which might be safe to act upon. Another area that can give practical concern is the so-called *budgetary estimate*. Even though estimates may contain the words 'subject to contract' – and they normally do – it can be worth considering the difficulty or confusion this term can cause. The giver of such an estimate sometimes offers it tentatively, often without checking that detailed examination has been given to it, to give the customer a rough idea, or an order of magnitude, of a likely offer which he might expect at some time in the future. The customer, on the other hand, takes it at its face value, passes it to his budget officer and gets next year's budget based upon it. Upon returning later to the salesman, both of them get a shock. What did the parties mean by 'budgetary'? Neither can agree, and in the meantime a thorough estimate has been carried out which yields a substantial increase in price. Consider inserting words such as

'Whilst this estimate is offered in good faith, it has not been based upon a complete specification or survey and has not been submitted to the company's full costing and estimating processes. Further discussion is needed before budgetary or financial reliance is placed upon it.'

These words may not be what the customer wishes to read, but they can save much misunderstanding later.

Choosing a library

We shall need, over a period, to establish a small library of books on contract and related commercial matters adequate to cover the kinds of situation which our particular line of business confronts us with. Foremost among these will be a good book on the law of contract, with which we shall probably need to become fairly familiar.

Choosing a good law book can be likened to choosing a good car. Not only should it contain all the necessary faculties to make it roadworthy and fit for its purpose, but it should handle well, 'feel right', and make us feel good when we spend time with it. This is more important than it might appear, since we ought to become familiar with its contents. That means spending quite a bit of time with it, which we shall only do if we find it enjoyable.

It is worth visiting a reputable law book shop and spending a considerable time examining all that they have on the chosen subject. Which volume do we feel we can live with? Which speaks our language? Which one is going to be easy to refer to in times of urgency and stress as well as when we have an hour or two to spare? Take a look both at the table of contents, to see whether it is broad enough, and the index to see whether it is comprehensive. Typically a good book of this kind will recite the principles of law in precise language, offer an explanation of each, and follow up with some illustrations from case law to develop understanding and, in some cases, to specify what is in fact the latest in judicial perception of a given situation.

Examine the date of publication, especially the latest edition date when it would have been brought up to date. Choose as recent a date as you can. Expect to pay between £30 and £50 for a good practical reference work. A practising lawyer's version might cost up to £200, but if you feel you need this level of detail, then you may be in territory where access to a law firm would be advisable anyway.

Summary

1. Set up a small law library that you can live with.
2. Remember that a contract may be written, verbal, or even implied by conduct.
3. It is best to have everyone sign an agreement, for the avoidance of doubt.

4. If you have to use 'offer and acceptance' be sure everyone understands the rules.

5. 'Agreement' is the act of agreeing in itself. The document called an agreement or contract is merely the evidence of it. This tenet can be useful when you find difficulty in processing 'the legal side' of a contract with your counterparty.

6. Whoever makes a contract can amend it or ignore it altogether *by agreement*.

7. Third parties are outside the scope unless they agree to be part of it.

8. Keep a lookout for casual language like 'budgetary estimate', 'heads of terms', 'heads of agreement'. Make certain everyone understands what is meant by such words and phrases.

3
Drafting contracts

One of the tasks with which we shall most frequently be concerned is that of drafting contracts, yet perversely there is very little published literature to show us how to do it. To some extent each person will develop his or her own techniques. It can be useful, however, to start with a framework of actions and to consider some of the tools of the trade, as it were. This saves a lot of time for the draftsman and also with colleagues.

Taking instructions

To solicitors in public practice, the taking of instructions might assume a fairly formalised process. To us, however, it is more likely to start with a telephone call stating that such and such a sales or contracts meeting is about to start, and can we please attend and draft something up. We may know little about the background and – more importantly – if our colleagues have little or no experience of contract preparation, they may know little about our own needs as contracts draftsmen.

It can help if we swiftly remind ourselves of the key tenets of contract law:

1. There must be agreement between the parties at the time they make the contract.
2. The terms must be reasonably clear.
3. There must be the intention to create a legal relationship.
4. There must be consideration or value given for goods or services provided.

We should try never to leave the meeting unless these key points have been addressed, or at least raised for further discussion.

Before arriving at the meeting it can be important to know who will be there. In particular, is this an internal meeting, or will the counterparty be there too? If it is not to be an internal meeting, we should try and get as much information as possible in advance, failing which we should listen a lot and say very little.

Who shall be the draftsman?

An early question to be resolved is 'who shall draft the contract, us or them?'

Almost without exception the bargaining advantage is with the side doing the drafting, so our initial reaction will be an immediate '*us*, please'. The initiative in drafting is valuable because it allows us to sit down at our leisure, and to carry out a full SWOT analysis of the proposed deal. By SWOT, of course, we mean

---

Strengths of our position.

Weaknesses of our position.

Opportunities to draft clauses in our own favour.

Threats from the other side.

When we finally produce our proposed contract fully drafted, it will be in our language, in a sequence of clauses and subject matter with which we are familiar because we drafted them that way, and with a battery of phrases which we ourselves will have designed, along with reasoned arguments to back them up in discussion.

To the other side, their first task will be to try and follow our logic. Then they will need to spend time and effort deducing what our arguments may be, what is 'reasonable' and what is not, and where the hidden risks are, in a document which they never planned in the first place. Even though the law may provide each party with a level playing field (for everything is negotiable) the team that drafted the contract is always playing at home.

Let us assume we have won that point, and the contract is ours to draft. What are the steps? There are no golden rules about taking instructions. We must devise routines which suit us best as individuals. To begin with, however, it is usually wise to try and keep things very simple. There will be time enough later to introduce the more complex legal principles if there have to be any. A check list of topics might look something like this:

1. Which are the parties to the contract? There will normally be two, but multi-partite contracts are quite lawful.
2. Do we know the official titles of each of the parties, and their addresses? Is each one a registered company, in which case we should ask for the address of their registered office? If a partnership or sole tradership, then we shall have to settle for the address at which business is done.
3. Is anyone trading under a business name other than their own? If so, what is it?
4. Which of the parties are promising to perform functions, such as to supply goods or to carry out services?
5. Do we need to take time writing full details of these goods or services and agreeing them between us, or are there specifications or other technical documents which we can incorporate by referring to them? Do we know what these specifications or documents are called, and whether there are any reference numbers or dates of publication to ensure that they are uniquely and correctly identified?

6.   Who is providing value or consideration and to whom? Is there a contract price or are there prices at all? If not, there must at least be a formula or a set of words whereby a value can be calculated later on with certainty. If we cannot establish this, then under English law there may not be grounds for a valid contract at all. We would merely be left with a series of voluntary undertakings.

7.   When is it intended that performance shall start? Is there a particular date or an event to which commencement can be linked? We might just state that it starts 'upon signature of contract' but we need to be reasonably clear about it, and whether it matters.

8.   Are there any preconditions to the contract starting, such as 'only if Party A wins the XYZ tender'? Are we clear about all of these, and is it going to be quite clear to each side when they have been satisfied (or 'purified' as Scottish lawyers would say).

9.   Is it quite clear what any 'deliverables' are to be? These may just be goods, but they might also be reports, instruction manuals, technical documentation, user guides, and 'bug-fixing' or fault correction bulletins released over a period. Deliverables can, of course, be substantial and complex, such as a complete factory fully installed and ready to commence production.

10.   What event or events constitute completion? Which of these events trigger payments and to whom? Are all the payments irrevocable, or do there need to be 'clawback' provisions in case one party never does fully complete its obligations even though it has been partially paid under the trigger arrangements?

11.   Is there a timetable of events? This might be linked to calendar dates or to the achievement of particular stages in the contract. Pay particular attention to interdependent events, e.g. 'Step 5 must start after Step 4 but it cannot commence before Steps 2 and 3 are fully complete, and neither of those steps can start until Step 1 is halfway through'. When in doubt recommend that a critical path analysis is done before final contractual arrangements are made. The outcome of this might determine how we need to draft our penalty clauses for delay.

12.   What could go wrong and when? How would it leave each party in turn if it did?

13.   Do we have all of this information available now, or must drafting proceed while some of the points are being resolved? Do we know which points have been settled beyond reasonable doubt?

A simple synopsis

If the instructions we have obtained are complex, or if we ourselves are relatively new to the game, we may find it helpful to produce a very simple summary or synopsis of the situation as we understand it. This should ideally be done very soon after the meeting, first, because it will be fresh in our minds, and second, because delay can lose impetus. If we take too long over it, there is even a risk that the other side will seize the initiative and publish a draft of their own. Such a synopsis might read a little like this:

At the meeting held last Friday it was agreed that:
- Parties A and B shall be parties to the contract.
- A will produce and install product X at B's factory.
- B will make ready a site to receive X and that site will be to the specification laid down by A.
- A will have the right to inspect the site, which must be to the correct specification and available to A at least six weeks before delivery of X is due, to allow A to complete certain electric and electronic cabling.
- A promises to install X and commission it, no later than 30 September.
- B shall have the right to carry out trials on the installed X for two months before accepting it.
- A will warrant the performance of X for one year following acceptance by B.
- The whole job must be installed and working by the end of the year.
- The contract price will be £999,999, of which 2.5% will be withheld by B until the warranty period is over. 10% will be paid by B upon signature of contract, a further 50% upon delivery of X, and the balance (less 2.5%) upon successful performance in the trials and acceptance by B.
- For each week of delay after the year end A will be charged 1% of the contract price up to a maximum of 10%, but not if A has been delayed by B's site not being ready in time, in which case B shall be charged damages at a rate to be agreed if as a result X is ready to be shipped and cannot be received by B without damage owing to unsuitable ambient conditions at the site.

Such a synopsis can be useful since by the very act of writing it, it focuses our mind on problems such as:

- Are the stage payments right?
- What is it doing to our cash flow?
- How and when are the damages for delay in B's site preparation to be calculated?
- What are the 'worst cases' in each event, and do we end up with A possessing more of the consideration money than they have earned?
- Are they a substantial organisation or ought we to insist on a bank guarantee for the money advanced, and so on?

Not all of these points may have occurred to the people who attended the original contracts meeting.

The first draft of the contract

Without waiting for some of these matters to be resolved we might proceed to the first draft of our contract. House styles in contract drafting vary from entity to entity. We need to choose our own. The merit of the following one is that it is simple and it also affords an opportunity to examine and consider each step of the process. The first page might read:

AGREEMENT

DATED THIS [fifth]

DAY OF [April 1999]

BETWEEN [The ABC Engineering Company Limited whose registered offices are at 123 Broadway, London SW99 1PQ (hereinafter referred to as 'A')]

AND [BCD Processing Limited whose registered offices are at B Works, Foundry Lane, Middle Bromwich, Central Midlands B99 1AA (hereinafter referred to as 'B')]

When is a contract an agreement?

First, it should be said that the terms 'contract' and 'agreement' are frequently used in commercial practice as if they were synonymous. To the purist, however, a contract may be established in various ways including its inference by conduct. A formal written document signed by all the parties actually evidences agreement right at the start, which is why most written contracts are headed 'Agreement' and are referred to as such.

Second, we should remember that the date is usually the last item to be inserted in a contract. It is normally established as the day upon which the last of the parties to sign actually does so. In this example it would be inserted on the front page, after the event and in clear handwriting, so that anyone can see at a glance when the agreement became operative. Other layouts which are quite lawful provide for dates to be inserted in the end page next to each signature. By examining that page and choosing the latest date, one reaches the same result.

Defining the parties

In the example given we have carefully designated the registered offices of each party. If one or other of them had been sole traders or partnerships we could not have done this. We would merely record their current business address. A registered company should always be described in terms of its incorporated name correctly reproduced and spelt. If either of them were using a business name in their dealings with us it might be appropriate to describe them thus 'The ABC Engineering Company Limited trading as 'Aardvark Automated Machinery' if that were their chosen name. Partnerships usually contract in the full forenames and surnames of all their partners, as does a sole trader, with or without the 'trading as . . .' suffix.

A word should be said about divisions of very large corporations which on occasion purport to enter into agreements as if they had a separate legal identity.

41

This is particularly so in the case of some large US entities, where an agreement may be drawn up as from 'The DEF Division of the FGH Corporation'. Such instances should be treated with care. If the FGH Corporation is the registered company of which DEF is merely a part, then FGH Corporation is the entity which one would sue, and the agreement should reflect this, even though its DEF Division is huge and has a good deal of freedom in signing contracts. On occasion it may be maintained that the DEF Division is empowered to act as agent of the FGH Corporation. This certainly makes life complicated. How does one call to account as agent an entire department? Such processes are relatively uncommon in English contract negotiations and corporate lawyers in USA will often gracefully concede if one's perplexities under the Law of England are tactfully expressed to them. Whilst large groups in the UK increasingly operate through company agency agreements for separate subsidiaries, there really should be a legally constituted entity which can be sued.

Defined terms and definitions

In these opening words and phrases we have introduced the concept of the *defined term*. ABC Engineering Company Limited may, in the rest of the document, be referred to for convenience merely as 'A' and BCD Processing Limited will be 'B'. Some authorities even suggest that on the signature page the legend appears 'for and on behalf of A' and 'B', respectively, although most draftsmen would consider that to be taking matters a little far, since it might be interpreted as making the individual signatories personally liable in various respects.

As the drafting progresses we shall find it convenient to introduce more defined terms. Each one saves us the trouble of repeating commonly recurring definitions. Drafting convention requires us to give each one a capital initial letter to distinguish it from the same word used in its basic meaning. For example, we may have defined in some detail the procedure for B to accept the product X from A. In such a case we could refer in one sentence to an undertaking that '. . . B will Accept X promptly upon request from A and A will accept debit notes issued by B covering excess costs chargeable to A.' One word, with two quite different meanings. Some draftsmen will construct a substantial set of definitions which they will often place early in the agreement. This helps to keep the wording brief and the meaning precise and consistent, but one has to take great care in interpreting the word 'Accept' as against the word 'accept', since the two will now mean different things.

The convention of capital initials is taken further than this. Where the context permits, they are used to designate the specific rather than the general. For example, 'the Directors' might be interpreted to mean those specific board members who have been defined as having a role to play in the agreement, whereas board members in general, including those of other companies, might be referred to as 'directors'. Likewise this particular contract may be referred to as the Agreement, whereas other legal documents may be referred to as 'agreements'.

In practice, the terms 'A' and 'B' might be considered a little terse to describe two companies and they are here used for simplicity only. Quite often functional terms will be adopted, such as 'the Supplier' or 'the Purchaser'.

Next may follow the preamble, which might run something like this:

WHEREAS:

1. B is desirous of acquiring from A the product known as X for value received.
2. A wishes to supply to B the product known as X and is willing to warrant its performance under detailed provisions contained herein.
3. A requires and B agrees that suitable and timely provision of a suitable site for X be provided by B.

NOW IT IS HEREBY AGREED AS FOLLOWS:

In law the preamble is not part of the agreement, as the final phrase suggests. It offers on the front page a very brief summary of what the agreement is all about. Occasionally a preamble may be used to introduce one or more defined terms, but these are more properly embedded in the body of the agreement. In the rare event of uncertainty of meaning of a kind which the preamble wording might clarify, the preamble becomes of some significance, but draftsmen should not rely upon this. The rule is always to make the body of the document clear and unambiguous.

The next step is to consider all the separate aspects of the document which will have to be drafted. Here it might be helpful to start a separate sheet of paper headed with each subject. Hence we might have up to nine sheets of paper headed:

---

1. Commencement

2. Work to be performed by A

3. Work to be performed by B

4. Deliverables

5. Acceptance Procedures

6. Warranties and Indemnities

7. Consideration

8. Provisions for Early Termination

9. General terms and conditions

If we take this approach we might number our clauses dealing with Commencement 1.1, 1.2, 1.3. Clauses having to do with the Work to be Performed by A would be numbered 2.1, 2.2, 2.3, and so on, throughout the document. This enables us to make insertions or deletions without having to renumber extensively. It also enables us to refer to a whole subject by citing Clause 1 or Clause 2, provided we make our intention plain.

A slight variant on this, which can be useful with very long agreements, is to have a 'Scope' section numbered 1 in the sequence. This might contain an initial clause 1.1 stating that 'Under detailed provisions contained herein the parties undertake the following:

> Clause 2   Commencement
>
> Clause 3   Work to be performed by A
>
> Clause 4   Work to be performed by B

and so on. It is sometimes considered desirable to place all the defined terms at the beginning of the agreement, in which case Clause 1 might be entitled 'Scope and Definitions', followed by

> Clause 1.1   Scope
>
> Clause 1.2   Definitions

A typical definitions clause might commence with the phrase 'Within this Agreement the following terms shall have the meanings ascribed to them in accordance with this Clause 1.2:

> 'The Work' shall mean performance by A of operations as specified in Appendix A hereto.
>
> 'Acceptance' shall mean demonstration by A in the presence of B that for not less than seven consecutive hours Product X shall correctly perform on site the technical functions in the manner specified in Appendix B hereto.

There might be a great many of these definitions, the need for which will occur to us progressively as we draft, which is why it can be useful to open up many sheets of paper. It is also useful to remember that not only can we place detailed technical and other documents within appendices, to keep them out of the way of the main document, but also – if they are very bulky – we can incorporate them by reference if both sides are agreeable, and provided we make our references unambiguous.

In the latter stages of drafting one may carry out refinements such as rearranging the definitions into alphabetical order. Try to minimise extensive clause renumbering. In complex drafting situations it becomes convenient to cross-refer by clause number. Much time can be spent re-examining the entire document to check that none of these reference points have become corrupted in their meaning after a major clause renumbering has taken place. Many word processing systems can now renumber paragraphs and clauses automatically, and some packages can even be set to renumber embedded cross-references at the same time. Beware, however: not every secretary or operator in a general business environment is familiar with these features in the software; and when software is misapplied to numbering systems, matters can get very confusing indeed.

At some point in the document it is usual to state that clause headings are for reference only and are not to be given any legal significance. This is to enable us to use titles for drafting convenience without having to stop and consider whether their effect might be to modify any part of the contract itself.

The drafting process

If we have elected to divide our agreement into parts 1–9 as suggested above, we may now commence detailed drafting within each part. To begin with it is advisable to use short, very simple sentences.

Try, if possible, to deal with every subject once only within the entire document. The more repetition there has to be, the more redrafting there is if that subject later needs to be amended. If you have word processing software which allows you to compile 'where used' and 'used in' tables this can be valuable. Should it be necessary to change the definition of 'Acceptance' during the proceedings, it can be important to spot all the places where that term has been used or referred to elsewhere in the document. Word processing software sometimes facilitates this cataloguing and selection if we use capitals for defined terms, such as 'ACCEPTANCE'. This may look ungainly in the body of the contract, but it is worth it if it helps us to get the drafting right.

It may be objected that many professionally drafted agreements contain long and complex clauses. This is true, but the main justification for such language is that it is familiar to the draftsman and/or that its meaning has been tested in law. 'Off the shelf' clauses can be very helpful to us. It is always our responsibility, however, to examine exactly what they mean and to satisfy ourselves that they really are applicable in each case.

L. W. Melville, in *The Draftsman's Handbook* (1985), offers specific points on drafting and interpretation, of which the following is a brief summary:

- Specify a commencement date where practicable within the text rather than relying upon an agreement 'commencing upon signature'.
- Check upon the signatories – that they have the appropriate authority to sign and to commit their entities.

- The written words will limit the interpretation of the contract. Only where words are ambiguous will extrinsic evidence be admitted to indicate meaning or intention.
- Generally words prevail over figures where they conflict.
- Construing a document is a matter for the courts, who will not necessarily be bound by the terminology used. Hence if we describe some peripheral undertaking as a 'condition' it will not preclude the court from assessing it as a mere warranty.
- Recitals, preambles and marginal notes are not part of the document but they will be taken into account to the extent that they may assist in arriving at the meaning or the effect.
- If a specific provision is expressed in considerable detail it will tend to exclude anything elsewhere in lesser detail which may be inconsistent with that provision. Some authorities suggest that because of this a draftsman should resist the temptation to specify in great detail except when it is clearly necessary.
- Where specific words are followed by general words such as 'and others' the general words will be limited to the class of the specific words.
- Where it is possible to resolve an ambiguity by construing the document against the interests of the party responsible for the ambiguity, that construction will be made.
- Words associated with each other are construed on a common basis.
- Repeated words are given the same meaning throughout wherever the document as a whole permits.

There is also a principle that the specific overrides the general where they conflict. Hence a group of clauses headed 'General Terms and Conditions' could be overridden in some respects by a further set entitled 'Special' or 'Specific Terms and Conditions' appearing in the same document. When drafting an agreement which contains more than one set of clauses, and possibly a series of documents included in appendices or by reference, it is good practice to include a clause indicating the priority which will be given to each in interpretation.

Termination clauses

One subject which deserves special drafting attention is the section dealing with termination, especially early or premature termination. In the normal way of things, the contract will run to maturity and may terminate when all rights have been exercised and all obligations fulfilled. It is worthwhile listing all the possible events that might prevent this happening:

- Bankruptcy or insolvency of any of the parties.
- Failure of B to provide a suitable site when required.
- Failure of A to deliver in an acceptable time.
- Failure to produce X to pass its acceptance tests.
- *Force majeure* beyond any date specified as being sufficient to terminate the whole contract.
- Failure of B to pay.

- Breach of contract by one of the parties.
- The serving and expiry of a fixed period of notice.
- Any other statement in any clause giving any party the right to terminate, implicitly or explicitly, before the agreement may have run its course.

We need to ask ourselves what the effect would be in each of the above cases:

- Have we correctly allowed for it in the drafting?
- Have we considered an order of priorities in early termination?

It may be necessary to preface some termination provisions with the words 'Unless previously terminated under provisions contained herein', or possibly '. . . unless terminated under provisions contained herein under Clauses 3, 5 or 7', as the case may be.

With very complicated contract logic it might help us to construct flow charts or algorithms indicating the various logical routes we may have to take in specified circumstances. Check these carefully with colleagues, and possibly with the other side too. Then draft the clauses and check that they agree with the diagrams. Consider some awkward coincidences, such as one of the parties becoming insolvent after having received a stage payment, when delivery has taken place but the acceptance tests are in the course of failure:

- Who owes how much and to whom?
- Who has the money and the goods, and who needs to have them?
- What are the risks of a receiver or liquidator taking possession, and where does that leave the other party?

Typing and checking the draft

When we have finished our draft, we should check it methodically for meaning and also for missed references. Whenever we cross-refer from one clause number to another, try reading that other clause together with the first to see whether both of them together still make sense. Whenever we refer to an appendix, does that appendix exist under the number or letter ascribed to it? Conversely, are there any appendices which by oversight are not referred to at all in the text? Have we incorporated any external documents by reference? If so, do we have a copy in the office ands are we quite sure that it has been correctly referred to, especially if there are different editions or updates?

The next step will usually be to get a version typed. Normally we shall have access to a word processor which will help us with spell checking and other devices, but needless to say the typescript should be carefully proofread before issue. It may still be convenient to start each typed section on a fresh page, and to allow plenty of room including wide margins for amendment. In most instances it is wise to give the draft not only a unique reference number but also a version number. We might be fortunate in securing agreement to Version One. It is more likely, however, that the negotiating session will stretch over several days or weeks. At times it can be important to know not only where we have got to in amendments, but also the various steps which got us there. It is not unknown for contract negotiations to stretch to 20 or 30 versions before signature if the project is large or complex. We need a procedure that will cope.

Obtaining signatures

What about the etiquette of obtaining agreement and signature? If agreement is secured at a joint meeting or meetings between the parties, then whichever party is providing the drafts will frequently offer typing and amendment support on the premises until agreement if reached. It is then common to draw up as many copies as there are parties. Each party signs and possibly dates the document on the signature page, and ultimately the same date – or the latest date – is inserted on the front page. Signature pages are commonly positioned after all the clauses of the agreement but before any appendices. Another practice is to place them right at the end of the entire document. Occasionally draftsmen will prefer a signature page followed by spaces for initialling or signing the appendices. It is also common, especially with overseas contracts, for each party to initial every page. This is particularly important if the document is not bound or paginated in a way which might make later substitution of pages difficult.

If the parties are not meeting, the procedure is a little different. Typically the proposer, who has carried out the drafting, sends two copies unsigned to the recipient party. This invites signature and return of both copies if all is in order. It is at this point that acceptance may take place and the agreement becomes binding. The proposer will then countersign both copies, returning one to the recipient and keeping one for himself.

If the recipient finds some of the clauses unacceptable he might counter-propose amendments. This he could do by marking up the proposed changes in manuscript. By convention lawyers tended to do this on the first occasion in red ink. Subsequent amendments used then to be made in green ink, after which a meeting or redraft might be appropriate. Nowadays most law firms have access to trained legal word processing staff, who will be familiar with 'red-line' features in the packages. They can automatically compare drafts, using document scanners to scan in amendments, which may also be received by email or diskette.

An alternative procedure is for the proposer to sign and issue both copies. This represents a more assertive bargaining stance, suggesting that he does not expect the other side to do other than to accept without demur. In each case the legal position is much the same, however, since the rules of offer and acceptance still apply.

Rectifying mistakes

It occasionally happens that, despite best endeavours, an agreement is entered into in error and the error is discovered quite soon after signature. Whilst this is potentially serious and the reasons for it should always be examined, the rules for mitigation of loss or damage should be remembered as well. A quick notification to the other party might mean that the matter can be halted before significant loss or damage is incurred.

Although we are at risk, in practice there are not so many situations where the other party can merely enjoy the benefits of an error made in good faith, to the first party's total discomfiture. In such circumstances time can be important in putting matters right. Delay becomes costly.

Summary

1. Remember the four basic rules for a valid contract:

   - agreement,
   - terms reasonably clear,
   - intent to be legally bound,
   - consideration or value.

2. Plan ahead of the first contract planning meeting.

3. Aim to be the party that drafts the contract.

4. Carry out a SWOT analysis: Strengths, Weaknesses, Opportunities, Threats.

5. Draft a dozen key questions to bring to the meeting. Aim to get them all answered before drafting begins.

6. Produce a simple synopsis. Have it checked by colleagues.

7. Adopt a 'house style' for written agreements, possibly along the lines indicated above. It will save time.

8. List the key subjects and start a separate sheet for each one.

9. Adopt a simple clause numbering system which minimises the need for renumbering when insertions or deletions are made. Use any software features to help you provided you have people who are familiar with their use.

10. Open a section for 'defined terms' and add to it as you proceed. Later it can be rearranged in alphabetical order. Always use capital initial letters for defined and specific terms.

11. Try and deal with each subject once only and in one part of the document. Keep each clause or sentence short and simple to begin with.

12. Place self-contained documents, particularly those of a technical rather than a legal nature, into appendices.

13. Include by reference any documents too bulky to bind into the agreement.

14. If many appendices or documents are referred to, indicate the order of precedence each takes over the others in the event of conflict of meaning.

15. Keep cross-references to a minimum. Make a list of where each one occurs, in case you later change any part of the referenced clauses, including their clause numbers.

16. Take special care of the termination clauses. Draw flow charts or algorithms when matters get complicated. Consider every combination of possibility, and where each one might leave the parties.

17. Be prepared to produce many versions of the draft agreement. Number each version consecutively as you go.
18. Adopt a standard method of presentation to the other party; refine it to suit your own environment and become familiar with it.
19. If an error does happen, be prepared to rectify it quickly.

4

Standard contracts: the 'boiler plate' clauses

In many contract negotiations one party or the other will table their 'standard terms and conditions for doing business'. What is the purpose of standard terms? Standard terms and conditions have several uses:

1. They can reduce the time taken to construct 'small print' so that the intending parties can concentrate on the central substance matter of the agreement.
2. They can reduce the overall work load on the party which offers them, since many clauses are repetitive and appear in identical or similar form over a number of different kinds of contract.
3. They can assist risk management and contract management. If we are confident that our standard set of clauses cover much of our exposure we may be able to authorise their use by representatives with less training in law and commerce, thus freeing our experienced contracts people for the difficult cases. We might even be able to nominate salesmen to sell on the standard terms without reference back unless the customer wishes to vary them. Likewise with purchase orders, where it is common to see the company's standard conditions of purchase printed on the reverse and referred to on the face.
4. A fourth use of standard terms is in the bargaining power they can give us:

'I'm sorry, we only do business on these terms.' 'I do not have the authority to vary them.' 'Only the Chief Executive can give authority for Clause 16 to be varied. He's out of the country for a couple of weeks.' 'Did you not say you needed the supplies by Friday? That's going to give us a problem. I may be able to offer a small discount for cash, but there's no way I can change that clause in the time available'

All are cries frequently heard across the negotiating table. Whether or not they are always strictly accurate, they create a line of bargaining strength and resistance to pressure which is not open to a counterparty who is obviously drafting bespoke clauses as he goes along. Indeed, one of the opening gambits in a contract negotiation is to be the winner of the contest 'your standard terms or ours?'.

Standard terms and conditions have one additional value to the Contracts Unit. They may enable us to table our standard situations, have the clauses drafted to fit them and then have them legally checked once and for all. They can then be printed (which always makes them seem as immutable as boiler plate) and implemented wherever practicable, leaving us free to concentrate upon exceptions and variations. A subsequent review every few years by a specialist lawyer is often quite sufficient.

Bargaining over the clauses

There is no one 'correct' stance to take on a contract clause. Where we draw the line will depend upon our bargaining strength, how badly we need the work, how risky a position we are in, and how aggressive the counterparty may be. To illustrate the point, let us examine some common standard clauses, and consider what they mean and how we might want to change them.

First, let us consider some of the *general* clauses which may set the framework for the agreement itself, and examine ways in which we might change them.

Choice of law and jurisdiction

Choice of law: 'The construction, validity and performance of this Agreement shall be governed by English law'.

Such a clause may be quite adequate if both we and our customer are in England or Wales and the contract is to be executed there. In such a case it would be implied anyway. We could probably get away with it if one of us were in Scotland, provided neither of us were a Scottish local authority or public utility.

If we are dealing overseas, however, the position may change radically. Our counterparty might for instance be French or German, American or Middle Eastern, and it may be to his advantage to cite his own local law. That may give us a problem if we have no legal expertise in that country's laws. Some legal codes require the definitive version of the agreement to be in the language of that country, adding a further burden upon us. Whoever has to accept a contract out of his home jurisdiction may suffer extra drafting and translation costs. If a dispute arises which cannot be settled amicably he has to face costs of lawsuits overseas. These can be high and can involve briefing foreign counsel, travel to attend meetings with the attendant language difficulties, travel and accommodation during the court hearing itself.

The law of contract is remarkably cosmopolitan, but there are important differences which may in any instance be material. This suggests professional overseas legal support at the outset if the contract is of significant value or risk. Bear in mind that a contract may be:

- Interpreted in accordance with English law and adjudicated upon in the English courts, or
- Interpreted in accordance with English law and adjudicated upon in the courts of Ruritania, or
- Interpreted in accordance with Ruritanian law and adjudicated upon in the English courts, or
- Interpreted in accordance with Ruritanian law and under the jurisdiction of the Ruritanian courts.

All of these options, bar the first, are more or less expensive if we are English, the more so if it involves paying for 'friends of the court' to attend and brief the judge on law he may not understand.

Custom suggests that in the absence of express agreement the effective law is the law of the country where the work is being done. But let us face it: the whole question may be subject to debate.

Compromises include choosing a 'neutral' code foreign to both parties. Candidates would be Swiss Law (Canton of Geneva), International Law Courts at the Hague, or, if in the USA, the laws of the District of Columbia.

Dealing with tax

Value added tax: 'Unless otherwise stated the prices in this Agreement are exclusive of value added or other sales tax', sometimes with the added phrase 'which will be applied in accordance with law'.

This is a useful clause that permits us to ignore the whole question of VAT (or any other sales tax which might arise) on the assurance that it will be applied whenever it ought to be applied. It is especially helpful if rates of VAT change, or if we occasionally find ourselves dealing with parties that are not registered for VAT.

Questions of publicity

Publicity: 'The Company's name shall not be used by the Customer in the endorsement of any project or in any other way or for any other purpose without the Company's prior written consent.'

This clause can be made to 'bite' either way, according to whether we want publicity or whether we do not. Maybe the deal is a prestige contract which we want to quote as a 'reference sell'. Occasionally, however, it may involve a humiliating climb-down – part of the deal being that everyone agrees to keep the details strictly confidential.

Better ways than going to court

> **Arbitration:** 'Any dispute regarding the construction, meaning or effect of this Agreement, or the rights or liabilities of the parties hereunder, or any matter arising out of the same or connected herewith shall, unless specifically provided herein, be referred to the arbitration in London of an arbitrator. The said arbitrator shall be appointed by agreement between the parties, or in default of such agreement, by the President for the time being of the Law Society of England and Wales, before the arbitration is commenced. Any such reference shall be deemed to be a reference to arbitration within the meaning of the provisions of the English Arbitration Act of 1979 or any statutory modification or re-enactment which may for the time being be in force.'

Arbitration involves a method of dispute settlement short of going to law. Many who have tried it, however, report that it is no less costly and may be just as time consuming. So this itself may become a bargaining point.

Alternatives to consider include strengthening the provision for mutual agreement on the processes. Try suggesting that as a first step two executives from each side who were not concerned in the contract should get together and try to resolve the dispute, failing which there shall be formal arbitration or recourse to law. Lawyers do not always favour this, but it can work very well and is not actually ruled out by the above clause. Whatever you do, however, try and include an express right to apply to local courts (whatever they happen to be) for any immediate injunctive relief to which you may be entitled. This could be a valuable remedy which you do not want to jeopardise.

One can always tinker with the appointment phrase, substituting the President of the Institute of Chartered Accountants, of the British Computer Society, or of any other suitable and reputable body. One can also select arbitration under the processes of the International Chamber of Commerce, or by the Centre for Alternative Dispute Resolution (ADR) in London. On the whole it becomes an issue only with the larger international contracts.

Getting it in writing

> **No waiver:** 'No waiver by either party of any provision of this Agreement shall be binding unless made expressly and expressly confirmed in writing. Further, any such waiver shall relate only to such matter, non-compliance or breach as it expressly relates to and shall not apply to any subsequent or other matter, non-compliance or breach.'

Clauses like this represent an endeavour to regulate informal conduct which can arise in the course of a contract. Verbal amendments may be made that never get recorded. Local management uses its initiative (often a dangerous thing with contracts!) and things get implied by the conduct or absence of conduct by one side or the other.

This clause attempts to say '*if it isn't in writing signed by both sides it doesn't mean anything.*' It also says that if one clause gets altered by due process, at least the rest of the document remains intact – rather like closing the watertight doors in a submarine.

It is good to have this piece of boiler plate. It is even better if its existence inspires a resolve to install a proper, written variation procedure whereby all amendments are signed by both sides, catalogued and filed methodically with cross-references, so that everyone can easily establish the text that currently applies.

Dealing with things we cannot control

> **Force majeure:** 'No failure or omission by either party to carry out or observe any of the terms or conditions of this Agreement shall, except in regard to obligations to make payments hereunder, give rise to any claim against the party in question or be deemed a breach of this Agreement if such failure or omission arises from any cause reasonably beyond the control of that party.'

Force majeure clauses, as the name implies, are attempts to mitigate the effects of events which are way beyond the powers of the parties to control. This example is rather broader in scope than many. Such clauses often restrict the definition of *force majeure* to specific events such as riots, civil commotion, acts of God, declarations of war between named countries, or industrial action by specified trades unions in specific respects. This may be safer, since the courts construe such clauses against the draughtsman, so that setting out all the circumstances is likely to lead to a wider sustainable clause. Examine your own risk exposure, and you will know how to negotiate the clause. The sentence excluding due payments from the scope of *force majeure*, is to guard against parties citing strikes in the accounts department, destruction of the bought ledger, or other 'obvious let-outs' to avoid or to delay payment.

Keeping lawfully in touch

> **Addresses:** 'Unless specified by not less than 7 days notice in writing by the party in question the addresses to which communications shall be sent shall be those shown in this Agreement.'

This is a good, sensible clause to avoid either side playing 'hard to get' when it suits them. Corporations can normally be reached at their registered office unless the contract specifically provides other arrangements. A well drafted contract will usually cite this address in writing in some prominent place within the document. Unregistered counterparties such as sole traders or partnerships do not offer such protection and it can be important to be able to serve due notice upon them without the responsibility of finding them after they may have moved. There may still be the job of tracking them down later, but at least the notice will have taken effect when served. Here is another which deals explicitly with postal and other more modern means of communication:

Notices: 'Any communications by either party to the other shall, unless otherwise provided herein, be sufficiently made if sent by first class post, postage paid, or by telex or facsimile transmission to the address of the other party specified for this purpose in this Agreement, or to any other address as either party may substitute by written notice to the other, and shall, unless otherwise provided herein, be deemed to have been made on the day on which such communications ought to have been delivered in due course of postal, telex or facsimile transmission.'

A clause such as this aims to remove some of the confusions of the 'Postal Rule' by making explicit the whole business of serving and receiving notices. It permits the use of instantaneous communication methods such as telex (now increasingly outmoded) and fax (almost universal). It would be quite easy to add a phrase permitting use of electronic mail systems such as the Internet provided each party has a modem and has furnished details of its email address. In some respects email is safer than fax, since a faulty fax transmission can occasionally result in missing lines of print at the other end.

A sound way of giving legal notices by fax would be to number each line of print in the margin and to indicate that one was doing so. A word of warning, however. At present there is little or no case law which deals with electronic methods of this kind. Consider inserting a phrase requiring key notices of that kind to be confirmed by registered post within a given period, if you feel it is important – or by fax confirmed by post.

Note the repeated use of the words *unless otherwise provided herein*. As we have already said, there is a rule that the specific overrides the general. Such phrases strengthen the application of the rule. It means that we can attach our standard clauses to other parts of the contract without amending them. Other parts of the contract which have been specially drafted will simply prevail if there is any contradiction. If we are going to do this, it helps if we call our routine clauses *general* terms and conditions, and the bespoke parts of the contract *special* terms and conditions so as to avoid any doubt. In large contract documents it is common to insert a clause spelling out the order in which various parts of the document take precedence one over the other.

Controlling special risks

Liability and indemnity: 'Except as expressly provided for herein the Company, its employees or agents shall not in any circumstances be liable for consequential, indirect or special losses or special damages of any kind arising out of or in any way connected with the performance of or failure to perform this Agreement.'

Clauses on liability and indemnity strike at the very heart of our risk management strategy, which is a subject in itself. Consequential or indirect damages are those losses which do not flow directly and immediately from the actions of the party in his performance under the contract.

For example, suppose a supplier of £50 widgets is late in supplying one special purpose widget under a 'time the essence' situation. As a result the customer defaults on a £50 million contract. Does the widget supplier pay £50 in damages or is he caught for the profit element in the £50 million? And what if the customer is sued for negligence by someone, arising from the contract upon which he defaulted and all thanks to the missing widget?

The standard clause starts from one end of the spectrum, protecting the widget supplier. Compromises may have to be reached. Liability for consequential loss might be restricted to 'the contract value' or some other figure. The buyer will doubtless keep bargaining for as much liability as he needs until the widget supplier exclaims 'That'll cost you £150 a widget' or possibly 'We cannot insure against that, and it could bankrupt us . Sorry, the deal's off!' However, consider also the Unfair Contracts Terms Act 1977 and, for consumer contracts, the Unfair Terms in Consumer Contracts Regulations 1994. Where the clause has not been individually negotiated, and is considered by the court to be 'unreasonable' it may be held void.

Now consider this clause:

'The Company shall exercise reasonable skill, care and diligence in the discharge of its obligations under this Agreement but in respect of any loss or damage of whatsoever nature and howsoever caused which in any way arises out of or is connected with the performance or non-performance by or on behalf of the Company of such obligations, the Company's liability and that of its employees and agents shall be limited in the case of negligence or default on their part and shall consist solely of performance or re-performance as the case may be by the Company of the obligation in question to the exclusion of all other liability. The Client agrees that it shall take no proceedings against any such employee or agent but shall look solely to the Company under the above provisions.'

The company in this case is a firm of management consultants, which at first glance may tend to confirm the suspicion that a consultant is 'one who borrows your watch and charges you a large fee to tell you the time'. It is, however, an interesting clause and worth analysing.

To begin with, what manner of subject is the consultancy being retained to advise upon? It is offering 'reasonable skill', where a 'skill' may be regarded as 'being familiar with a particular science, trade or art, combined with the ability to apply oneself in those areas with ease and dexterity'. Reasonable care is that level of attention which an ordinarily prudent person would apply in all the circumstances. 'Reasonable diligence' means much the same thing, though this term tends to be used by American law firms, and American law dictionaries tend to have scales of diligence ('high', 'low', 'due', etc.), whose distinctions are not immediately clear. This might be relevant in dealing with a Wall Street firm, or if you are retaining an adviser in a international takeover bid. Reasonable skill and care is implied automatically in contracts for services under the Supply of Goods and Services Act 1982. It is therefore better to rely on an express clause.

If we are looking for more dedication than that of any ordinarily prudent person with certain specified skills and experience, we might insist upon a 'professional' degree of skill. This takes it up a notch or two, especially if there is a clearly defined profession involved.

The next part of the clause deals with what we may do if things go wrong. It is telling us that damages as such are 'out'. If the consultants get it wrong, our remedy is to make them come back and put it right. If the nature of the study is highly speculative or 'state of the art', or if we have a reputation for being highly litigious with advisers who fall out of favour, this may be the best we can obtain. The argument for this phrase may be that consultancy of certain kinds is a highly intimate affair requiring a superior degree of mutual trust and respect, such as one might obtain between responsible senior colleagues with a common objective, and that litigation is irrelevant or unnecessary (*'You should not want to take us to court. Your interest lies in allowing us to complete the work, which is what we wish to do anyway because of our reputation. And it is because of our reputation that you are hiring us'*). One or two US firms even claim that they will only consider as clients those organisations which they have vetted as 'acceptable'. Nice work if you can get there. We have to consider to what extent we accept this concept, and that will depend upon the circumstances. For instance, a contractor may not exclude liability of personal injury or death, for non-consumer contracts, if they are caused by negligence. So ensure that this is clear in the contract.

The final part of the clause deals with the protection of the consultancy's staff or agents. We may not sue them. Under privity of contract it may be argued that these people are protected anyway, since we have no contract with them. There are, however, some instances where a right of action might lie – they might have committed a tort against us, such as negligence – and this would be a way of getting at them and indirectly at their principals. Do we want to prise open that route, or are we content to let it lie?

'The Customer shall, during and after the period of this Agreement, keep the Company and its employees and agents indemnified against any claim, demand, action or proceeding by any third party, arising out of or in any way connected with the performance or non-performance, whether negligent or otherwise, and howsoever a head of damage may be formulated, by or on behalf of the Company of its said obligations, brought or instituted against the Company, the Company's Affiliates, or its or their employees or agents.'

Because of the potentials and uncertainties of tort actions from third parties, some contractors draft additional clauses whereby the client indemnifies them against third party actions arising from the contract. This might seem extraordinary and impertinent. Consider, however, the plight of a small consultancy offering services to an oil major on a rig in the North Sea which it shares with many other, fairly litigious, multinational groups. Such a clause might be their only effective protection. If they get sued, they immediately enjoin the oil major in their defence and (with luck) a large corporate legal department takes over the defence on behalf of both of them.

A special word about indemnity clauses. If they are drafted against *us* we need to take care, especially if they are for very large sums, or unlimited. Sometimes they will be insurable risks, in which case we should consult our insurers before accepting them. Usually the party which accepts an indemnity clause against them will insist that a rider be attached: '... *provided that [we] shall be informed forthwith of any claims arising hereunder and shall have the right to take control of the defence thereof including any related settlements*'. This ensures that he who pays the piper shall call the tune, as regards the extent of the damage he may have to suffer. It is particularly important where there is a risk that the other party, against whom the claim is actually being made, may consider that to settle without a fight represents a 'soft option', since whatever he agrees with the plaintiff will be at our expense. It may be to everyone's advantage to settle without an expensive court action – but the decision needs to be ours!

Controlling who the other party is

Assignment: 'Except as otherwise provided in this Agreement, neither party to this Agreement shall without the previous consent in writing of the other party assign this Agreement or any rights or obligations thereunder.'

Under common law a contract could not be assigned and so this clause once would have been unnecessary. Equity has to some extent modified the position. Specific rights such as debts due can be assigned unilaterally, and rights held by a person who dies are automatically assigned to the personal representatives.

Similar considerations can arise in bankruptcy, and there is some statute law which applies here too.

Stated simply, this non-assignment clause is inserted by those who do not wish in any circumstances to find themselves in contract with any parties other than those with whom they made the original contract. This re-establishes the common law position and is not often the subject of much debate. Occasionally a rider is added '. . . *save for the purposes of amalgamation or reconstruction*', which allows for internal assignments within a group of companies.

Making the document all-embracing

> **Entire agreement:** 'This is the entire Agreement between the parties in relation to the subject matter hereof and the terms and conditions incorporated therein shall not be contradicted by evidence of any oral, other or prior agreement, understanding, representation or warranties express or implied.'

This is a powerful clause for the seller because it says in effect '*what is not in this contract does not exist between us*'. A common objection is that the parties have been talking together for weeks, the salesman has been busy extolling the virtues of the product, building up expectations, and of course all those understandings are part of the reason for buying. The seller, if he is wise, will reply with the argument that nothing is more dangerous in contract work than the 'verbals' which no one can remember with clarity. An hour setting them down in writing as part of the agreement will be time well spent. Put like that, it can be hard to resist.

Another 'variation' clause

> **Variations in writing:** 'No amendment or variation of any of the terms and conditions of this Agreement shall be binding upon the Parties unless approved by both of them (or 'all of them').'

The main thing here is to ensure that it is approved.

> 'For the avoidance of doubt, the words 'this Agreement' shall be taken to mean these General Terms and Conditions together with any form of agreement with which they are incorporated.'

This is the handle which attaches this group of clauses to other parts of the agreement.

Keeping things 'watertight'

Unenforceable terms: 'The invalidity, illegality or unenforceability of any term or condition of this Agreement shall not affect the validity, legality or enforceability of any other term or condition of this Agreement.'

This clause provides more 'watertight doors'. Should part of the agreement be found to be contrary to law (it might be judged 'unreasonable' under the Unfair Contract Terms Act, or in restraint of trade, or flawed in some other respect) there is an added likelihood of the rest of the document surviving, provided the judge decides that it is still capable of legal significance.

Termination clauses

Now let us consider some of the situations where we might 'want out' of a contract rather quickly for a variety of reasons:

'Notwithstanding anything to the contrary expressed or implied elsewhere in this Agreement, this Agreement may be terminated (without prejudice to the other rights of the parties) by written notice:-'

This opener to a set of clauses seeks to 'clear the decks' for termination and asserts itself above other parts of the contract, unless there are some specific clauses elsewhere which clearly take priority. So to continue:

'. . . forthwith by either party in the event that the other party being an individual, or where the other party is a firm, any partner in that firm shall at any time become bankrupt or shall have a receiving order or administrative order made against him, or shall make any composition or arrangement with his creditors, or shall make any conveyance or assignment for the benefit of his creditors or shall purport to do so, or if in Scotland he shall become insolvent or any application shall be made under any Bankruptcy Act for the time being in force for the sequestration of his estate, or a trust in deed shall be granted by him for the benefit of his creditors.'

Here are all the various ways in which an individual or a group of partners can get into financial trouble in a recognisable form. As soon as this happens they become more or less incapable of managing their own commercial destiny and – potentially – of honouring any engagements they may have with us. Their receivers, managers or trustees in bankruptcy are only interested in getting at their assets to satisfy the claims. Often that is all they are allowed to do. This sub-clause permits us, if we wish, to stop at once, to avoid putting any more effort into the project, and to join the queue of creditors in the hope of getting paid something.

And in case the other side is a company, the following clause may be used:

> '. . . if the other party being a company shall pass a resolution, or the Court shall make an order, that the company shall be wound up, or if a receiver or manager on behalf of a creditor shall be appointed, or if circumstances shall arise which entitle a Court or a creditor to appoint a receiver manager or administrator or which entitle the Court to make a winding up order.'

Should the counterparty be a US company, then a reference such as '. . . or if in the USA, Chapter 11 of the appropriate legislation is instituted . . .' might be inserted.

Other general termination clauses might include:

> '. . . (termination) by the Customer in the event that the Company fails to carry out the work specified in this Agreement [save for *force majeure* as defined herein] and that such failure by the Company remains unremedied for [14 days] after receipt by the Customer of written notification of such failure by the Customer.'

The words in square brackets, of course, may be varied.

> '. . . (termination) by the Company in the event that the Customer fails to make payment as required hereunder.'

This last clause might be expanded to include 14 days' opportunity to rectify.

Use of delivered work

'Other than for internal test and evaluation purposes the Customer shall not, without the Company's express permission in writing, put into use the results of any work carried out hereunder before payment has been made in full. Where stage payments are made, use by the Customer of the results of the work shall be restricted to those parts which directly relate in an identifiable manner to payments already made, and no licence of the intellectual property rights in such work is granted to the Customer until such payment is made.'

The appropriateness of a clause such as this will depend upon the nature of the goods or services being provided. It is more often found in the supply of 'state-of-the-art' technology, where there are stage payments and where the deliverables are provided in stages – each perhaps with separate test procedures.

A supplier may be concerned to protect himself against a customer who will find it feasible to use that which has been delivered, even though it does not fully comply with the specification in the contract, and will then have no incentive to cooperate with the supplier in his attempts to rectify and improve so that final payments become due. In high technology contracts full cooperation between buyer and seller may be essential to the seller.

Intellectual property rights

Computer software suppliers, or licensees of patents or other items of technology, will commonly insert a clause such as this:

'The copyright and other proprietary rights in or relating to any document or other material produced or supplied by the Company or otherwise made available to the Customer shall under the terms of this Agreement remain vested in the Company. The Customer is hereby granted a non-exclusive royalty-free licence, but without the right to sub-license, to reproduce solely for its own internal purposes documents software or other material produced or supplied hereunder in which the Company has proprietary rights.'

The effect of this clause is to allow the supplier to retain ownership of the software or other rights, including the right to supply them elsewhere, whilst allowing the customer to use them internally. If the fee being charged reflects this, it may be quite appropriate. If the customer has commissioned a special-purpose system to put him ahead of his competitors, however, he would be unlikely to agree to it. A problem which has to be recognised is that much software contains general purpose sub-routines which are used many times in different systems. No supplier of such routines could grant the copyright to any one customer.

Set-off clauses

'Set-off' is the right to settle an account which is owed by netting it against any balances which may be owed the other way, so that one merely pays the difference. Standard clauses are often included defining each parties rights to set-off. This happens especially when one or more of the parties are large organisations which may well be buying and selling with one another at the same time. A word of warning. In a recent legal case, *Stewart Gill Ltd* v. *Horatio Meyer & Co, 1992*, it was held to be *prima facie* unreasonable – and therefore unenforceable – to include in a company's terms of business a clause excluding or restricting the right of set-off.

Points such as these are well worth discussing with lawyers when periodically reviewing standard contracts.

Summary

1. Standard contract clauses can save time.
2. They can help manage risks.
3. They can give bargaining power.
4. Each clause, however, is negotiable if we wish it to be.
5. General standard clauses can deal with
   - Legal code
   - Tax matters
   - Publicity
   - Arbitration
   - Making certain everything is in writing
   - Things outside our control
   - Special risks
   - Assignment rights
   - Keeping things 'watertight'
   - Terminating early
   - Bankruptcy and insolvency
   - Acceptance and use of delivered work
   - Intellectual property.

5

Procurement matters

It is sometimes said, in simple terms, that purchasing or procurement is concerned with getting the right goods or services, in the right quantities, to the right specification and quality standard, in the right place, at the right time, and at the right cost. Before examining some of the finer points of how best to make this happen, let us briefly consider a typical purchasing cycle as it might occur in an average factory employing systems and paperwork which are commonly found.

The purchasing cycle

1. A need arises for some goods or services.

2. Someone checks to see whether there are any in stock. There are not.

3. A decision is made to obtain the supplies. A form will be filled in, usually termed a 'purchase requisition'. Information given on the form will include:
- quantity required,
- description or specification,
- part number, if there is one (which normally specifies the article precisely to designs and drawings),
- delivery address,
- date required,
- any special instructions,
- budget or account code chargeable with the cost.

In 'classic' buying situations the supplier identity and the price is not known with certainty at this stage, so a maximum value might be stated for the order in total. This amount would be within the requisitioner's signing authority. In practice it may happen that the requisitioner has technical knowledge which may influence the source of supply, so that a supplier and expected price might be included. In companies where this happens a lot, the forms may allow for a supplier name and address to be nominated.

4. The purchase requisition then goes to the Buyer or the Purchasing Department, the requisitioner usually keeping a copy. The Buyer examines it and may refer to any records indicating where this item has been bought before.

Was the source of supply satisfactory? Were there any problems? How many suppliers are there in the market and what is known about each? If the item has an engineering specification, it might be necessary to check whether the item has been modified or upgraded in any way since the previous supply, so that the suppliers are given correct details. The Buyer might also have access to stores in the company not available to the requisitioner. Is the item in stock somewhere else? Could it be manufactured within at less cost than the suppliers would charge? Is there an under-utilised plant which could produce the item more economically? 'Make or buy' decisions are not always made by the Buyer, but it is an option which needs to be reviewed.

5.   The Buyer then obtains quotations. After due consideration of the relevant factors a Purchase Order will be issued to the chosen supplier. This is an offer to do business and it will have contract terms included with it, often printed on the back. Since it may be accepted by written acknowledgement or sometimes by performance it is a valuable document not unlike a blank cheque. Purchase orders are frequently kept locked away. Most are numbered sequentially, either at the time of printing or by computer when they are being issued. Sometimes they will bear a notice stating that they are not valid until they have been numbered and signed. They will also state that the number must be quoted in consignment notes, invoices and other documents as a safeguard against the acceptance later of unsolicited goods.

   A copy of the purchase order will be held by the Buyer and additional copies may be sent to the requisitioner, the Accounts Payable unit and the Goods Inwards unit at the intended point of delivery. In a large factory or warehouse organisation there will be many different goods inwards bays, and there may be detailed instructions to the supplier as to exactly where and how to present the goods. Failure to comply may mean that the goods will be rejected out of hand. This may be necessary to prevent widespread confusion and delay, in areas where there is heavy goods traffic most of the time.

6.   In due course the Supplier is ready to despatch the goods. He will post a despatch note to the Buyer indicating the quantity, the item, and the order number, as advance warning that delivery is about to occur. He may have been instructed to send a copy to the Goods Inwards point as well. With the goods themselves will be a packing note containing the same information.

7.   Upon arrival the goods will be identified by the packing note, which is retained. Sometimes the carrier is provided with a copy which might be signed off and stamped 'Received Unexamined' unless checking has been done at once.

8.   Goods Inwards, having satisfied itself that the materials were indeed ordered and are expected, will check the quantity, making a note of any shorts or overs against the packing note and the delivery note. They might also check against their copy of the purchase order. Any variations will be noted.

9.   Quality inspection will then take place. Any faulty goods will be placed in a 'quarantine store' while a decision is being made as to whether to return them or to rectify them on site. The sound materials will be booked into a store from

which the factory may draw and use them. Alternatively they may be passed directly to the requisitioner.

10.   The paperwork then begins to flow. Notification or receipt of the sound material will be passed to the Buyer and/or the requisitioner, possibly in the form of an endorsed despatch note copy. Accounts Payable might also get a copy to help them accept the invoice when it arrives. If the inspector has rejected any material, a reject note might be issued to the same units. Someone, possibly a production superintendent, will decide whether the reject material can be rectified on site and, if so, whether the cost should be recovered from the supplier. Otherwise, the Buyer may contact the Supplier to arrange for correction.

11.   There will then be a procedure for checking invoices on arrival. Were the goods ordered? Were they all present and correct? If so, the invoice will be cleared for payment. If not, payment may be delayed while the Supplier is asked for a credit note for the appropriate amounts. In these days of value added tax it can be important to insist upon correct paper flow in this respect.

This, then, is the sequence of events that we set in motion when we place an order. A traditional buying system is outlined in Figure 4.

The purchase order

Let us now examine a typical purchase order in greater detail, and discuss some of the small print that we may expect to find on the back of it.

First, there will be the *Supplier's name and address*, sometimes called the 'Vendor'. There may be an address to which invoices have to be sent, and a *delivery address* which might include a specific factory gate or bay number. The *purchase order number* is usually prominently displayed, and the Supplier will be instructed to quote it in all documents and communications. Although the *purchase requisition* is not the business of the Supplier, it is sometimes included for administrative convenience. In some systems, copies or extracts from the requisition are forwarded to the Supplier as part of the order. Whilst this can be convenient and may save labour, care needs to be taken that requisitioners and suppliers do not start a practice of 'dealing direct' so that copies of the requisition, informally made available, begin to be treated as if they were legally binding orders. Not only is it bad buying practice, but ultimately the requisitions could be deemed to have legal effect even though they have not been properly authorised and have no terms and conditions attached to them.

Often there will be a space headed '*Contract number*' or '*Blanket order number*'. With regular suppliers it may be convenient to negotiate long term supply contracts, often with advantageous discounts and special terms and conditions. These then form the basis of the legal relationship, and the purchase orders become merely documents for calling off quantities and directing them to the right places at the right times. 'Blanket order' is a term sometimes applied when budget authority has been cleared up to a total aggregate sum, and both Buyer and Supplier have been told they have authority between them to arrange fulfilment up to that limit and no further. Language is not standard, however. Each use of these terms needs to be defined somewhere.

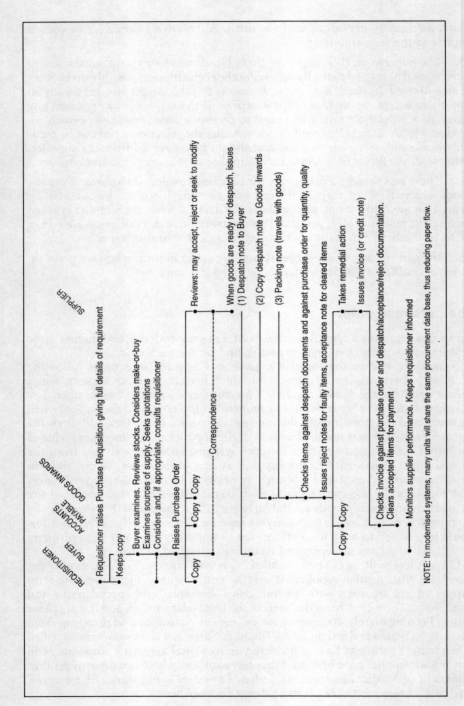

Figure 4 Outline of a traditional buying system.

There may also be boxes to define carriage details (method, and who pays), payment terms (net 30 days after receipt of invoice, perhaps), and any particular carrier or route of shipment which is intended. With international trade there are designations described in full detail within 'Incoterms' (1990 version). Some of these are briefly dealt with below.

c.i.f.: Price includes carriage insurance and freight at Supplier's expense to the delivery point.

c & f: Price includes carriage and freight (possibly because the Buyer has an insurance policy which covers goods in transit anyway).

f.o.b.: Free on board. Here the price just covers delivery and loading on to a named vessel at a specified port. 'F.o.b.' is never used in air freight.

ex works: Here the Buyer collects from the factory.

The body of the purchase order may look similar to an invoice. Typically it will contain the following items:

- *Item number*, a useful reference point for telephone or other queries.
- *The quantity ordered.*
- *The unit* in which the quantity has been expressed (cases, packets, weight in lb, kilos, or volume in gallons, litres, etc.).
- *The part number*, if applicable.
- A *full description*: this may include the Supplier's part number, if known, and sufficient narrative to identify what is required. It may be convenient to cite other documents rather than fill the form with many lines of detail.
- *The unit price* will then be quoted, reflecting any quotation which may have been obtained, and indicating any discount that will be applied.
- *The amount* (indicating the currency if appropriate).
- *The total amount* will be given at the foot of the document, indicating the value of the order as a whole. There will also be a space for signature by a person authorised to commit the company for that sum of money.
- *Delivery date*. This may be a date applicable to the whole order, or else there may be a column in which dates can be separately specified for each item. For the avoidance of doubt it may be considered wise that any critical or 'time the essence' dates be specifically labelled as such.

If the buying organisation is a registered company, then by law it must declare its correct registered name and number, indicating the country of registration. It must also bear the registered number and its correct registered office. It may be convenient to include the VAT registration number, although this is not obligatory.

To ensure that any terms and conditions are included in the document, it is important to have wording included on the face of the order similar to this:

'This Order is subject to all terms and conditions appearing hereon, on the reverse side hereof, and/or attached hereto.'

This notice needs to be in clear bold type so that no one can claim that it was not reasonable to have noticed and read it. On the reverse of the order it is common to have printed General Terms and Conditions of Purchase – also in clear bold type which is easy to read. These are automatically incorporated into the offer which is being made to the Supplier. Under the contract drafting rule whereby the Specific overrides the General, it is allowable to amend the printed clauses by indicating any changes to them in clear unambiguous language on the face of the order. It is also possible to attach any specific or special clauses to an extra sheet or sheets, and to attach those sheets to the order. When doing this, however, it is wise always to indicate that one is doing it by means of a sentence within the Order details. It is also wise to indicate how many sheets are being attached, and to number the sheets (e.g. 'Sheet *n* of *m* sheets'). If we fail to do this, and any of the sheets become detached, the Supplier may claim that he never saw them and part of the contract becomes invalid, or at least very difficult to establish.

It is usual to see a further statement somewhere on the order:

> 'The Purchase Order Number must appear on all invoices, packing notes, packages and correspondence. Packing notes are required with each consignment.'

Sometimes this notice is placed next to the place where the purchase order number appears to avoid other reference numbers becoming confused with it.

General conditions of purchase

Let us now consider the various clauses which may appear as 'General Conditions of Purchase' on the reverse side of the order. As with many contracts, it is not unusual to commence with some key definitions:

> **1. Definitions**
>
> In these conditions and in all documents related to the Purchase Order:
>
> 'The Company' means [full, correct name of buying company] and any of its subsidiaries.
>
> 'Supplier' means the person, firm or company on whom the Order is placed.
>
> 'Order' means this Purchase Order and any amendment thereto placed on the Company's behalf by a duly authorised Officer.
>
> 'Articles' means all goods, materials or services to be supplied in accordance with the Order.

Such a clause defines the commonly used terms in a form which makes them comprehensive and less likely to be avoided on legal technicalities of a kind which no *bona fide* party is likely to have intended. There may be cases where they need amending, however, and no one should accept them merely because they are 'standard'.

---

2. The Agreement

(i) These conditions and any issued in accordance with Clause 15 ('Additional Clauses') shall represent the entire agreement between the parties and shall take precedence over any terms and conditions issued by the Supplier at any time. No additions or qualifications to these conditions shall be valid unless they have been issued by the Company as a formal Order amendment signed by the Company's relevant authorised staff.

This clause is part of what is sometimes known as 'the battle of the forms'.

The 'battle of the forms'

When two organisations endeavour to do business with each other, each using their own standard paperwork, whose conditions prevail? Those in the purchase order, or those in the Supplier's quotation which probably say exactly the same thing in relation to the *Supplier's* conditions?

There is case law on this subject, taking the matter right down through the standard paperwork, even as far as rival statements on packing note copies stamped, in effect:

'Accepted subject to our conditions which take precedence over all others.'

Who prevails? It is probable that the last party to wield the rubber stamp wins the game. It is not a game which sensible buyers and sellers should play, however, since the ultimate winners in such proceedings tend to be the lawyers.

Even though purchasing paperwork tends to be drawn up as if the Buyer decides everything, the processes of Offer and Acceptance leading to Agreement apply in just the same manner as in every other kind of contract. The way to avoid battles over forms is for someone to pick up the telephone, draw attention to the conflicting paperwork, and to start a discussion which will result in words that each side can accept, and agreement upon how the forms will be amended to reflect this.

An exchange of letters is often the best way to cover the matter, possibly with a reference number which can be quoted on all future orders. The only way in which purchase orders may differ from other kinds of contract is the very specific manner in which they may define those company staff who have buying authority.

If we are the Supplier we *must* be certain that we are dealing with authorised buying staff – not just the requisitioners – or else with a director or other officer of the company who clearly has ostensible buying authority. If in doubt check it with the company secretary. That is why a clause such as 2 (i) above can be so valuable from the Buyer's viewpoint. It is an essential control mechanism for him against unauthorised purchases.

Order amendments

A word may need to be said about order amendments. Unless special commitments have been made by the Supplier, he will be under no obligation to execute amendments unless he separately accepts them. This principle applies no matter what the standard paperwork states.

> **2**(ii)   The Order number given on the Company's Order must be quoted on all documents and on all correspondence related to the Order.

This makes the quoting of the order number a contractual obligation. What penalties the Supplier would suffer for breach might depend upon the circumstances. If there were delay in payment which could be attributed to this cause the Supplier might find it difficult to sustain a claim for damages upon late payment.

> **2**(iii)   The Order including these conditions and any appended documentation shall be deemed to be a contract when the earlier of the following occurs:
> (a)   the Supplier issues an acknowledgement to the Company accepting the Order, or
> (b)   performance is commenced by the Supplier.

Whilst this clause in the main states the law of contract, it can be useful to have it so stated so that there can be no doubt. In particular it specifies that as soon as the supplier has begun work there is a contract, whether or not the Buyer is directly aware of the commencement. This reflects the fact that much purchasing and supply work is routine, and need not depend upon the strict observance of exchange of documentation. From the supplier's viewpoint it might be important not to commence any work on 'time the essence' Orders until someone has decided whether they are clearly capable of fulfilment within the time. This is especially necessary if – as is often the case – pressure is being put for rapid action, possibly a 'job start' in advance of the official paperwork.

---

3. Quality

(i) The Articles shall conform and shall continue to conform to the quantity, quality and specification stated in the Order and any relevant British Standard (or agreed equivalent) and shall be fit for the purpose intended as indicated by the order.

(ii) The authorised representative of the Company and/or of the Company's customer shall be entitled, subject to reasonable notice being given, to inspect the Articles at the Supplier's premises.

Clause 3(i) specifies that the Articles shall be fit for their purpose, which is one of the implied warranties of the Sale of Goods Act 1979. It also allows the Buyer to specify what that purpose is. In addition, it provides that if any BS number applies to the Article then it shall be supplied to the standard indicated. This is a valuable provision for the Buyer if he elects to use it. Correspondingly, it will not trouble the Supplier *unless* the specified purpose is not one for which the Article was designed. In such a case the order should not be accepted without discussion and possible an escape clause drafted.

In **Clause 3(ii)** the right to inspect work in progress is a usual provision. For the Buyer it can help to guard against faulty workmanship, and also give some protection against the supplier who is running late and who is not reporting the fact. From the Supplier's viewpoint, he needs to be certain that work is not proceeding in a part of the factory that contains secret processes or prototypes unrelated to the work in question.

---

4. Delivery and title

(i) The Articles shall be delivered by the Vendor at its own expense in accordance with the Order to the address specified by the Company.

(ii) The Supplier shall pack and mark the Articles in a manner suitable for storage in a normal office environment, unless requested otherwise by the Company.

(iii) Times stated in the Order for delivery of the Articles shall be of the essence.

(iv) Title in the Articles shall vest unconditionally in the Company upon delivery thereof in accordance with this Clause 4, in the case of delivery by instalments then title shall pass on each instalment.

Clause 4(i) is the standard delivery instruction where the supplier delivers at his own cost to the delivery address specified in the order. If one of the other forms of delivery were chosen, such as 'ex works' this would be specified on the face of the order, possibly with the works address in the 'delivery address'. In such cases attention would have to be given to the procedure for goods inwards inspection.

Clause 4(ii) is a clause suitable for office equipment. In an engineering environment the words '. . . normal works environment . . .' might be substituted.

Clause 4(iii) is interesting in that it seeks to make 'time of the essence' whenever a delivery date is specified. A watchful supplier would be likely to challenge this if he is not supplying standard items from stock. Although it may be argued that no diligent supplier should accept a delivery date which he cannot be confident of meeting, there is also the question of what level of commitment from him is reasonable in each case. If the Buyer is in a line of business where times really are critical and where any reasonable supplier ought to realise this, such a clause embedded in the general conditions might suffice. In other instances, however, it would be wise for specific attention to be drawn to the existence of such a clause, on the face of the order.

Clause 4(iv) is powerful in that it is weighted in favour of the Buyer. As soon as the Articles are delivered – and before they might have been paid for – they become the property of the Buyer. If the buying company then becomes insolvent, the liquidator may sell the delivered goods for whatever he can get and the Supplier joins the queue of unsecured creditors for whatever dividend is ultimately paid. Such a clause might be accepted when the Buyer is a substantial organisation; otherwise he may expect to have it challenged.

Title, risk and settlement

There are three elements of commerce which need to be borne in mind when reviewing this type of clause: title, risk and settlement. In the absence of agreement to the contrary, the law is as stated in Chapter 8, which deals with the sale of goods and services. Often, however, the law is modified by specific clauses which will tend to reflect the 'muscle' of the party which has drafted them.

In a neutral situation, if such a thing exists, *title* or ownership of goods may pass at the moment when – having been inspected – they are paid for in full. Until that time, they may be the property of the seller. He therefore bears the risk of them being lost stolen or damaged, for which he may insure. In a totally Buyer-dominated situation, however, title may pass upon delivery, or even earlier when materials are assigned to the product.

Risk may remain with the supplier until after delivery and subsequent acceptance by the Buyer, and the seller accepts risk of loss or damage right until full acceptance and settlement – for which he may insure. Clauses stipulating this are not unknown, especially when advance payments are made early in the contract and before initial deliveries have been made.

At the other end of the spectrum, the seller may retain ownership of the goods until all payments have been made, including any retention money that may be held during a period of trials or warranty of performance where the contract says so. Risk, on the other hand, may pass as soon as the product leaves the factory, for which the Buyer is obliged to insure and to demonstrate to the seller by producing evidence of cover.

Settlement, the third element, may by agreement occur at any of these times: at the very outset, with a clawback provision in the event of non-performance;

right at the end of the proceedings when all outstanding obligations have been discharged; in the middle; or by any sequence of part payments linked either to milestones on the project or else to specific periods of time. Typically both buyer and seller will have blanket insurance cover which can be adjusted to reflect either the normal risk pattern in the business or else specific cover for specific contracts.

Sometimes these matters merely reflect what is included in the price. At other times they can represent hazardous exposures to one side or another, typically when the counterparty is – or might be – in difficult financial circumstances.

A liquidator can be prevented from disposing of goods in his possession whose title is held by another company. Conversely, he may be able to obtain possession of goods whose title he has if they are held by someone else, even if they have not yet been paid for. Yet he may not have enough money to pay that party for them. It is in matters such as this that risk adjustment needs to be made. Credit insurance or indemnity can be arranged, but it is not cheap.

---

5. Prices

All prices quoted by the Supplier shall be fixed and deemed to include all costs of packaging.

This clause may not cause difficulty to the Supplier provided he has merely given a price with no strings attached. If his standard quotation form has conditions to the contrary, a negotiation is likely to be triggered off.

---

6. Rejection and defects

(i) Any Articles found not to be in accordance with the Order may be rejected by the Company and returned to the Supplier at the Supplier's risk and expense.[1] Upon rejection, title in the rejected Articles shall immediately revert to the Supplier. The Supplier shall promptly repay to the Company any moneys paid by the Company in respect of the rejected Articles and shall deliver to the Company replacement Articles without undue delay. The Supplier shall invoice the Company for the replacement Articles in accordance with the Order.

Clause 6(i) needs to be read together with the notes above on title, risk and settlement. The Buyer is distancing himself from what are, in effect, unsolicited goods. He is requiring the right to ship them off his premises, where they may be creating congestion. The cost of this is to be with the Supplier, whose property they now become once again, as also the risk of loss damage or destruction. Moreover he is asserting that this is not to be used as an excuse for undue delay in supplying the right Articles.

[1] Under the Sale of Goods Act 1994 this may be invoked even for slight defects.

6(ii) Unless otherwise agreed and in the absence of any other period agreed between the parties the Company may, within a period of twelve (12) months following acceptance of the Article(s), return the Article(s) to the Supplier, in the event of the discovery of a defect which arises from defective workmanship, design or material or which represents a non-conformity with the Company's Order. The Company shall return the Article(s) as soon as reasonably practical and at the risk and expense of the Supplier. The Supplier shall repair or replace the Article(s) free of charge without delay and the balance of the above-mentioned period at the time of defect shall recommence upon acceptance of the replacement Article(s).

(iii) The benefit of Clause 6(ii) may be assigned by the Company to its customer.

The existence of clauses such as this on the back of purchase orders should serve to remind every supplier to take the time to read them carefully. The supplier is in effect warranting all his supplies for 12 months from initial acceptance, plus any rectification time that might arise. The acceptability of this undertaking will depend upon the kind of supplies. Manufacturers' motor parts often carry this kind of warranty, and for standard engineering articles it may well be appropriate. An enterprise supplying the kind of materials which can be graded accurately on inspection might wish to vary the clause, as also might a supplier of highly technical, state-of-the-art technology.

Note the right to pass this undertaking to the ultimate customer, which from the Buyer's viewpoint may be quite reasonable.

7. Termination
(i) The Company may terminate or suspend this Order at any time in whole or in part by issuing a notice to the Supplier. The Supplier shall conform with the requirements of the said notice but shall be entitled upon provision of full details and supporting evidence within thirty (30) days of receipt of the said notice to submit a claim to the Company for reasonable unavoidable loss directly suffered by the Supplier by reason of such termination or suspension.

(ii) The Company may at any time without prejudice to any other remedy and without notice terminate this Order if the Supplier is in breach of any of its obligations hereunder. In the event of such termination the Supplier shall not be entitled to submit a claim for any loss.

(iii) The Company shall be entitled without prejudice to any other remedy to terminate the Order if the Supplier fails to deliver the Article(s) or any part of them on the date(s) specified in the Order, and (a) return at the Supplier's risk and expense any Article(s) previously delivered which cannot be used as a result of the subsequent failure to deliver and to recover from the Supplier all moneys paid by the Company in respect of the Article(s), and (b) recover from the Supplier any additional costs reasonably incurred by the Company in procuring replacement Article(s) from an alternative Supplier.

Clause 7(i) may be one which many suppliers can live with. It follows the law of contract and allows for *quantum meruit* payment if the contract is suspended unilaterally by the Buyer. A writ of specific performance is ruled out, but provided the Supplier can produce evidence, and provided he mitigates his loss, he should not be greatly out of pocket.

The risks to him in a break clause such as this lie in circumstances where evidence of cost is not going to be easy to supply, or where commitment of resources, and the achievement of profit, is unevenly spread throughout fulfilment. In these cases he should prepare to renegotiate. Since the imposition of this kind of cancellation is entirely outside his control, he needs to consider the implications carefully. He may argue that there is no reason why he should be out of pocket at all, and may even seek a liquidated damages clause of a kind which recompenses him for loss of profit. Much will depend upon the circumstances.

Clause 7(ii) may appear reasonable, but it does give a Buyer the upper hand. How many obligations has the Supplier agreed to in the order and all related paperwork? How minor or accidental a breach could give rise to termination? Unless some special conditions of urgency exist, ought there not to be some notice period, and the opportunity to rectify within that period? These are bargaining points to consider.

Clause 7(iii) reflects the 'time the essence' nature of this kind of purchase order, and as such should normally be treated with caution by the Supplier whenever he is not supplying standard articles from stock. If a delivery date has been set by mutual agreement and after due discussion all might be well. The danger in these situations from the Supplier's viewpoint is that purchase orders are standard, routine documents which are often merely scanned by relatively junior staff in the sales order department before they are accepted and processed.

Clause 7(iii) offers perhaps the greatest risk, since there is no maximum level of damage. It can be particularly damaging where the only other sources of supply offer higher quality, higher priced equivalents. It is, however, a damage quite properly claimed in the event of a serious breach leading to termination. A sharp sales contracts officer might seek to limit his liability to a stated figure commensurate with the nature of the job.

7(iv) Either party shall be entitled to terminate this Order forthwith by notice in writing if the other party shall be adjudged insolvent or bankrupt or shall be unable to pay its debts as they fall due or shall make an assignment for the benefit of its creditors generally or have a receiver appointed for it or any of its property or assets or if it shall discontinue or abandon or dispose of the whole or a substantial part of its business or shall have a petition presented or a resolution passed for its winding up other than for the purposes of amalgamation or reconstruction, or a notice is issued convening a meeting for the purpose of passing any such resolution.

Either party is here given the option to terminate at once by written notice if the other party has indicated formally in any of the specified ways that it might not be financially sound. The option rather than a certainty is significant, since a key supplier may well be able to deal with a receiver or manager in a way which will preserve the contract and his own fulfilment of it on sound terms.

> **7**(v) If the Supplier has submitted a claim under Clause 16 (*force majeure*), of which the period from the date of notification exceeds three (3) months then the Company may, without prejudice to any other remedy, terminate the Order at no liability for costs or expense.

In this set of clauses the *force majeure* definition has been drafted quite widely. Clause 7(v) offers the Buyer a way out if the stated likely period of delay is long.

> **7**(vi) Any termination or suspension pursuant to this Clause 7 shall not affect the accrued rights of either party.

Such a clause allows the significance of the various classes of termination in Clause 7 to be perceived by a reading of the clause rather than an examination of all other relevant documents.

> **8. Changes**
> The Company may at any time by Order amendment make reasonable changes to any of the requirements of this Order. Within thirty (30) days of the issue of any Order amendment, the Supplier shall notify the Company and provide supporting details of any change in price or the time for delivery occasioned by the Order amendment. If no such notification is received by the Company within the stated period then no changes in price or time for delivery shall take place.

Like so many standard purchasing clauses, **clause 8** is appropriate and even mutually convenient where the Supplier is making regular supplies of standard, specified articles. It is especially applicable in a factory situation, typically under 'just in time' arrangements, where the Supplier may be as much involved in the Buyer's production schedules as some in-house departments of the Buyer.

Where it can become dangerous is with the 'special purchase' item, or in the development contract. Then it can be important for both sides – and certainly for the Supplier – that a proper change or variation order procedure is agreed. Such a procedure involves active participation by both sides.

9. Documentation and invoices
 (i) All Advice Notes and Certificates of Conformity shall be submitted in duplicate by the Supplier. The original shall be sent by first class post to the Company's Procurement Department and the copy shall accompany the Article(s).
 (ii) Valid invoices shall be sent by first class post to the Company's Accounts Department and shall be payable within the period agreed following date of receipt subject to satisfactory discharge of the Supplier's obligations hereunder.
 (iii) All documents, including Advice Notes, Certificates of Conformity and invoices must state the Company's Order Number; any documents which fail to do so shall be invalid and shall be returned to the Supplier.
 (iv) It is essential that any invoice from the Supplier must relate only to one Order. Failure to observe this requirement will result in the invoice being rejected and returned to the Supplier.

Clauses 9(i)–(iv) specify the documentation procedures of the Buyer. A supplier who wishes to get paid promptly will adhere to them carefully. Even though they may appear bureaucratic by the standards of small companies, a large organisation – especially a manufacturing plant – finds this sort of documentation essential. It is likely that over the next few years increasing use will be made of electronic document transfer, which will cause such procedures to be revised.

10. Confidentiality
The Order and any related information shall be confidential and shall not be disclosed by the Supplier to any third party for any purpose without the prior written consent of the Company (which shall not be unreasonably withheld).

Non-disclosure clauses vary in intensity according to whether official secrets are involved or merely a wish for normal discretion. Some authorities include a rider '. . . save and to the extent that such information shall become in whole or in part a matter of public knowledge other than by a breach of this clause'.

11. Indemnities
 (i) The Supplier shall indemnify the Company against all loss or damage occasioned by any act or omission of the Supplier, its servants or agents whilst on the Company's premises or by the failure of the Supplier to comply with its obligations under the Order or occasioned by the use of the Article(s) except where such loss and/or damage is caused solely by misuse of the Articles by the Company.
 (ii) Except where the Article(s) are manufactured to drawings provided by the Company, the Supplier shall indemnify the Company against any liability, loss, damage and/or expense which may be incurred by the Company as a result of any infringement by the Article(s) of any registered design, patent, trademark or copyright of any third party.

As stated in Chapter 4, all indemnity clauses need careful scrutiny. Many including those above are insurable risks. A safe rule is always to declare such clauses to brokers or underwriters for an opinion when they first arise. Usually when an underwriter refuses to cover a clause, one has justification for seeking its deletion or amendment. Often the brokers themselves will offer helpful advice on how to obtain a necessary amendment. It will be an unwise counterparty who is unwilling to listen in such cases, since he may be exposed too.

Of course, a Supplier with a poor claims record will find cover difficult just like everyone else. It is important that procedures are in place to minimise chances of claims.

---

12. Title

The Supplier warrants that it has the unfettered right to supply the Article(s) which to the best of its knowledge infringe no third parties' rights. Unless otherwise stated the Company shall have a royalty-free licence to use, re-sell, or let the Articles for any purpose.

Infringements of intellectual property can be serious. Not only might they be expensive, but legal remedies exist which can, in some circumstances, involve the searching of premises and the impounding of infringing articles and documents giving evidence of their use. The Supplier is safest who only supplies materials to which he himself has copyright, patent or other title.

Anyone selling on materials whose title is owned by another needs to scrutinise his own documents of purchase. Sometimes detailed instructions for relicence are provided in a form convenient for copying forward to end-users. Once again, an experienced buyer will not challenge these, any more than a prospective sub-tenant of a property will challenge covenants laid down by the freeholder. He will, however, want to know what they are (see also Chapter 8).

---

13. Spares and Support

(i) The Supplier shall maintain and supply Articles for a minimum period of five (5) years from the date of Acceptance by the Company of the last of the Article(s) to be provided hereunder. Such Articles shall be provided at prices and delivery periods no less favourable than those agreed for this Order.

(ii) Prior to ceasing production of the Articles the Supplier shall, upon giving six (6) months' notice undertake to deliver to the Company without charge all necessary drawings, licences, manufacturing information, tooling, documentation, etc., to enable the Company to manufacture or procure the manufacture of equivalent Articles.

Clauses of this kind are industry-specific. Not every supplier will be in a position to accept clause 13(i) without qualification. Five years is a long time, and inflation rates can vary greatly over such a period, as also can material supply times.

Clause 13(ii) may need to be checked against any intellectual property documents to ensure that such a right can be conveyed. 'Tooling documentation' may be easily photocopied and passed across. But 'tooling and documentation' might give a problem if more than one customer were to ask for it.

---

14. Items on loan

All material issued free to the Supplier by the Company or by any third party on the Company's behalf shall remain the property of the Company or the third party as the case may be and any material remaining unused on completion shall be returned in good condition to the Company together with any scrap materials. The Supplier shall be responsible for the condition and safe custody of free issue material whilst they are in his possession and shall adequately insure against such risk. The Supplier shall use such materials solely in connection with the Order. Waste of such material arising from bad workmanship or negligence of the Supplier shall be made good at the expense of the Supplier. Any free issue materials found by the Supplier on receipt thereof to be defective shall not be used but shall be returned immediately to the Company for replacement. Any drawings or other such documents supplied with the Order shall be returned to the Company upon completion of the work.

This situation commonly exists in manufacturing. The Supplier in this case may be able to arrange insurance cover to be extended to goods in his care as well as goods in his ownership. The Buyer has here the protection of being able to reclaim all of this material in the event of an insolvency – provided he acts fast and can identify it.

---

15. Additional clauses

The Company reserves the right to include in the Order additional clauses to reflect the relevant contract between the Company and its customer.

Arguably this is an unnecessary and slightly misleading clause. Any purchaser may include any clause in a contract that he wishes provided it is communicated to the other party and accepted. The clause may serve as a reminder that some clauses attached may not be within the power of the Buyer to amend.

---

16. *Force majeure*

Neither party shall be liable to the other for any delays in performance or failure to perform any of its obligations hereunder where such delay or failure arises due to reasons beyond its reasonable control, subject only to sub-clauses 7(i) and 7(ii) above. In every case the appropriate party shall immediately notify the other party in writing of the said event and defining the expected effect thereof submit to the other party the necessary information to verify and substantiate such claim.

In some industries the definition of *force majeure* would be more tightly drawn. Here the parties are agreeing that neither will gain from the *force majeure* affecting the other, however they define the term 'reasonable control' when the time comes. Clause 7 offers the injured party a way out.

---

17. Waiver

No failure, delay, relaxation or indulgence on the part of either party in exercising or partially exercising any right hereunder shall operate as a waiver of such rights.

This avoids occasional lapses to be implied by conduct as being an amendment to the order.

---

18. Sub-contractors

(i) The Supplier shall neither sub-contract (except as is customary in the trade) nor assign any of its obligations hereunder without the prior written approval of the Company. Such approval shall not relieve the Supplier of any of its obligations hereunder.

(ii) The Supplier shall be responsible for ensuring that its sub-contractors are bound by and shall observe the terms and conditions of the Order.

It is important here to understand the difference between a sub-contractor and a supplier, and if in doubt to establish the difference, since interpretations vary. In general a *sub-contractor* is a party who *takes over a part of the contract* that the prime contractor has undertaken or is about to undertake. He is executing a part of the work which is peculiar, or at least specific, to that prime contract. A *Supplier*, on the other hand, is one who is making available under a contract or order *goods or services of a kind which are also available to others*.

---

19. Statutory requirements

The Supplier shall observe and ensure that the Article(s) to be supplied comply with the Statutory Rules, Orders, Directives or Regulations in force at the time of delivery.

This is an important clause in view of the environmental protection laws which are now in force. Care needs to be taken in supplies outside the UK and especially to overseas governments where additional laws or orders may apply.

---

20. Law

The Order shall be deemed to have been placed in England and the construction, validity and performance thereof shall be governed by English law . . . [possibly with the addition] . . . with the English Courts having non-exclusive jurisdiction.

This is a usual clause. The significance of stating that the order is deemed to have been placed in England is that the jurisdiction of the English courts is established. Some clauses state this in so many words.

Using fax and electronic mail

As business methods progress the use of facsimile and electronic transmission methods in procurement may be expected to develop. One way of ensuring that the legalities are established is to provide Suppliers with a set of background clauses and procedures which, by prior agreement, are deemed to apply.

Where business is being done by fax it is helpful to add a standard rider — possibly on the cover sheet- indicating that faxes may fade over time, and that they may be preserved by taking a photocopy. Likewise, some authorities indicate confidentiality on their fax cover sheets, indicating that they should not be shown to third parties. If wrongly transmitted, they should be destroyed or returned to the sender. It is unclear, however, whether the last sentence could be enforced, since there would be no legal relationship between the sender and an incorrect recipient.

If intricate contract clauses are faxed, consider whether to use fax transmission sheets bearing lines numbered from 1 upward consecutively in the margins. If a line gets garbled or missed altogether, the recipient will be aware of it. Try always to ensure that hard copy confirmations are sent.

Summary

1. Be aware of the essential features of a procurement cycle.
2. Examine how your own organisation adheres to these.
3. Consider how any deficiencies might be handled.
4. Check that the correct company details appear on documentation.
5. Confirm that Standard Terms and Conditions of Purchase are used.
6. See that they are referred to in bold capitals on every purchase order AND printed clearly on the reverse.
7. Ask how often they are reviewed and by whom. When were they last examined?
8. Do goods receivable staff have instructions not to accept delivery notes with contract clause statements on them?
9. Does anyone have authority to buy on the telephone or verbally? How are they controlled?
10. How are the three elements title, risk and settlement dealt with? Do purchase order standard terms reflect this?
11. Is fax or email used? Are there adequate safeguards?

6
Managing risks

What is risk?

According to Daniel L. Schneid in *The Financial Executive* (January 1984):

> Risk is a Four-Letter Word. It is one of those words that people use without having a clear-cut meaning for it. And it is not uncommon to see someone try to get away with its definition by telling us how it is measured.
>
> Large amounts of money and time are spent to measure and reduce risk because **risk is always present in a decision**. We can sound sophisticated in the classroom or in a textbook if we substitute the word 'risk' for *ignorance, stupidity, negligence, forgetfulness, blunder, mistake, error,* or *Act of God*.

So risk is clearly here to stay, and a key objective in contracts management is to help manage the risks of the enterprise. What are the key risks in business and how might they be managed?

Managing business risks is essentially the same as managing personal risks. Let us examine how many of us do this quite simply in our private lives, and then consider how the same principles might be applied in business.

Managing risks in life: A personal case history

When we first leave school or university, one of our early goals will be to pass our driving test. Money is tight. Our first car is unlikely to be valuable; indeed it might be something of an 'old banger'. We might consider ourselves lucky if we have enough money to get it through its MOT, taxed, insured and on the road.

We are obliged by law to carry third party insurance, to protect other people from the risks of meeting us on the high road. We should like to carry comprehensive insurance like our parents probably do. It is quite the best way to control one of the main risks in our life – that of losing an asset that we should find hard or even impossible to replace. Now, however, we find a problem. Because of our youth and inexperience, the best comprehensive premium we can obtain comes to considerably more than our car is worth, and probably more than we can afford anyway. So what do we do?

Each person will decide this for him- or herself. A possible outcome is that we shall buy as much protection as we can afford, and take a chance on the rest. Third party cover we have to take, and this is the largest part of the premium. Fire and theft will cost us a little more, but might be worth taking, if we can manage it. The 'comprehensive' element we might decide to forgo for two reasons:

(a) the extra premium is so close to the value of the car that it makes sense to carry the risk ourselves, and/or
(b) we cannot afford the extra premium but we need the car to go to work. Thus it is less of a risk to take a chance on not having an accident and keeping our job, than not to use the car and to lose our job at once.

Of course if we do *not* need the car for work, we might choose to manage our risk in another way by not insuring and using the car at all until we are better off.

As we progress in life, our attitude to risk changes. Money becomes less difficult. We become experienced drivers. It may become practicable to insure our car fully. Indeed, we may have a more valuable car, so that it makes more sense to insure it fully.

We now have more options to consider. Should we pay the top premium for 100% cover, or dare we take a 10% reduction and pay the first £100 of each claim? Our decision will be influenced by how easily we reckon we could find the extra £100 in an emergency if we had to. The wealthier we are, the more able we shall be to take probabilities into account, knowing that if fortune is against us we shall still survive.

Alternatively, we might be inclined to pay above the odds for a good insurance deal as we perceive it, such as the chance to preserve our no claims discount for an extra 10%, so that even some accidents which are our own fault need not hurt our pockets.

Our personal tastes and attitudes to risk will vary too. Some of us will stay with 950 cc engine vehicles to keep the costs, the risks and the premiums down. Others will adopt higher risk profiles, for a variety of reasons, and may progress to the GTI models regardless of premium. We might tell ourselves that it is a necessary cost in projecting the image we need to succeed in life, and we may be right.

Taking matters still further, we might achieve such wealth and the lifestyle to match that we elect to buy and run a Lamborghini regardless of the fact that – with our record for reckless driving – the best cover we can get is third party all over again. If we are prudent, we shall only do this when we have the cash resources to fall back on should disaster strike.

As we progress through life, we learn to apply risk management principles to situations we barely thought of when we were young: life assurance, pensions, sickness and accident exposure, nursing home care in our old age, even our funeral expenses!

So what are these principles in a nutshell? First, let us consider risks which we might share with professional risk takers such as insurance underwriters.

Insurance checklist

1.   Which risks do we have to insure by law, whether we wish to or not?
2.   Which risks are so easy and inexpensive to cover in relation to the protection offered, that insurance is an obvious 'yes'?
3.   Which risks are so difficult or expensive to insure against that we might have to accept them as part of the hazards of staying in business?
4.   Which risks fall between these extremes, so that we might consider taking a share of the hazards ourselves in return for lower premiums? And how much of these hazards would we feel comfortable with?

In business situations Employers' Liability cover falls right within Category 1, and close behind it comes Product and Public Liability. These items deal with our responsibility to our staff if certain categories of claim arise, and to the general public and to our clients or customers as a result of our business activities. For all practical purposes we *have* to carry these classes of cover, in the same way as we have to insure our motor fleet to 'Road Traffic Act' standards. As it happens the premiums are commonly quite low in relation to the levels of protection offered (unless we are in a hazardous line of business) but that is immaterial – we have no choice.

Within Category 2 might come fire insurance for our offices and factories, fairly inexpensive depending upon the standard of fire detection and alarm that we may have, and the nature of the material we store. Often Business Interruption cover can also be relatively inexpensive. This is the cover we may obtain to insure us against the other risks arising from fire or flood disaster: the cost of accommodating staff elsewhere, of obtaining and training new or temporary staff to replace those who may have been injured, the lost orders, the lost markets, the lost profits, covering whatever period we consider it would take us to recover from the disaster.

Category 3 might include office contents insurance. It is not unusual for companies above a certain size to be self insured for theft of office furniture or contents, apart from cash or specified valuables. The premiums can be relatively high in relation to value.

A more difficult risk to manage in Category 3 is Professional Indemnity ('PI'). PI insurance covers an organisation for errors, omissions or other kinds of negligence in respect of any professional duty it may have to customers or clients; a consultancy gives unsound advice; a member of staff is dishonest as a result of which the customer suffers loss or damage; libel or slander is unwittingly committed; key documents are lost or damaged. PI insurance is not always easy to obtain and costs can be high. Compulsory deductibles are common, as also are ceiling figures for the levels of indemnity. A poor record of claims can disqualify, since it is an area of high risk to underwriters. A manufacturing company may have little need for this cover. A firm of solicitors or surveyors, or a consultant surgeon, might be out of business without it. Other enterprises may fall between these extremes, but difficult choices are sometimes made. The best professional advice from brokers can be vital.

Category 4 situations can arise in many areas. Motor fleet insurance is an obvious field where choices can be made, ranging from 'fully comprehensive' for the smaller fleet to 'third party only' for fleets above a certain size, which is quite usual as a conscious choice. The costs of insurance are deemed higher then the risks of vehicle write-offs and the company can afford to be self insured in the non-statutory areas of cover. In these cases it is usual to carry 'stop loss' insurance so that any losses above a certain total figure are indemnified by underwriters. This is to guard against risks such as a very bad year for claims, or a major disaster at the factory engulfing most of the company car park areas at a time when they are full.

An important point to be made about risk management is that the way to control the risk will depend upon the size and character of the organisation as much as upon the risk itself. The largest multinational corporations in the world tend to be self insured for virtually all of their hazards. Even the statutory risks are sometimes placed through an insurer merely to ensure legal compliance, and are backed by a full indemnity from the corporation to the underwriter. This keeps the premiums very low indeed, since they are little more than handling charges. Insurance underwriters are in business to make a profit. If we are big enough and smart enough we can keep some of this profit for ourselves. For instance, sovereign governments are smart enough seldom to insure at all. We the taxpayers underwrite the risks they take, whether we like it or not.

Handling contract or project risk

Let us now turn to all those risk areas which cannot be covered by insurance and which probably represent the greater part of our concerns as contracts managers. What is the likelihood of *this particular contract* producing profit? What are the dangers of it leading to loss, and what can we do about it?

There is probably nothing in contract risk management to compare with a rating system built up by us and our project managers, over a period, reflecting the profile of typical jobs which have led to loss or other kinds of exposure, indicating the common or recurring factors which internal post-mortems have revealed to us as being dangerous to our particular enterprise. Since it can take several years, much managerial effort, and a good deal of corporate humility to produce a really effective rating system learning from mistakes, let us start with those areas which we might examine at the outset.

Some organisations have found that a simple questionnaire, with brief answers, can provide in a few pages enough information to give the experienced director or senior manager all he or she needs to 'sense' the risk levels, and to make sound decisions when a contract proposal is being examined. Such a project risk questionnaire is presented in the following.

--- **Questionnaire** ---

The project itself

1. Do we understand the nature of the project?

2. Have we examined the principal milestones during the life of the project, as we foresee it, and their effects upon how we conduct ourselves? Have we submitted them to the PRAMKU test? Are our intended obligations to the customer Precise, Realistic, Accepted, Measurable, Known, and Understood by all concerned including the prospective customer? 'Measurable' has the sub-titles: Quantity, Quality, Time and Cost.

3. Have we examined the following likely or possible events and considered their implications:

- Preparing the proposal
- Offer and acceptance of tender
- Getting the contract agreed and signing it
- Starting work
- Allocating staff and equipment
- Buying supplies and equipment not available internally
- Moving people and material to the Customer's selected location
- The commissioning or testing processes which, when successful, will oblige the customer to accept and pay in full
- Any residual period during which there will be an obligation to rectify faults or sub-standard performance at no cost to the customer

4. How do we establish what event or series of events establishes that we have carried out our obligations?

5. Does this give us the right to demand payment in full? If not, how do we qualify for full payment? Is this reasonable, or does it allow for an unreasonable customer to delay settlement unreasonably?

6. How sensitive are our obligations to variations in dates for key items to be completed? Are 'time the essence' situations matched by 'time the obligation' undertakings? If the dice are loaded, in whose favour?

7. If there should be penalty or liquidated damages clauses for delay, what are the risks and exposures to us? Have they been analysed, and are they acceptable to us?

8. Do we have sub-contractors or suppliers on whom we are crucially dependent to satisfy our obligations to our customer? If so, are they as bound to us as we are to our customer?

9. Are we reliant upon our customer for certain facilities or other contributions: site access, suitable ambient conditions to receive our equipment, adequately trained staff to liaise with our own? Provision of key information in a manner to which we can relate? Are there conditions in the contract which allow for this, so that failure on his part can exonerate us from any blame or liability for our own failure to perform?

10. Are we obliged to comply with given safety standards? Has this been built into the specifications and are we being adequately rewarded for compliance?

11. Are specific staff members mentioned in our proposal or tender? If so, is it clear whether substitutes will be accepted in the case of illness or other unavailability, or are we being made totally dependent upon their continued availability?

Sales considerations

1. In our tender, are the reasons why our service surpasses those of our competitors adequately stressed?

2. If we succeed, will additional markets be opened to us? (it may be worth taking a higher risk for higher long-term rewards).

3. Is the proposed price keen enough to win the contract? If not, and if it cannot be improved upon, why are we continuing with the bid?

4. Is the cost to the customer, and the likely timescale, clearly presented?

5. Is sufficient pricing information presented to enable the customer to make realistic choices, without revealing cost make-up data which might be confidential to us?

6. If there are completion dates imposed by the customer. are we imposing acceptance dates by which the bid must be awarded to be compliant?

7. Will there be a legally binding offer document indicating for how long our offer will remain open, and stating whether or not it is subject to contract?

8. Are we citing our own standard terms and conditions?

9. If not, have theirs been examined? Has a risk analysis process been applied to them, and what is the considered outcome?

10. If the tender is to be a legally binding offer, have all appropriate management been warned in advance? Have legally binding obligations been obtained in a suitable form from any key suppliers or sub-contractors?

11. What is our perception of the personal relationships between our own key people and those of the prospective customer? Are the company cultures compatible? Does it matter if they are not?

12. How about our own relationships with key suppliers and sub-contractors? Will this be a contract that runs smoothly, or are there likely to be many misunderstandings?

13. How about third parties, such as professional advisers — especially those retained by the customer? What is known about them and the circumstances of their appointment? Are they likely to be supportive of customer/supplier relations in the interests of getting a fair contract duly completed, or is it perceived that their success will be judged by how 'tough' they are seen to be upon us and our suppliers? Is any allowance being made for this, if it is relevant?

14. Are we reliant upon cooperation from the technically qualified staff of the customer? Will there be a contract clause specifying this need in precise terms, and the obligation to provide it?

15. Is the working environment of the customer such that modifications or enhancements to whatever we provide are likely to be essential for him? If so, is he aware of this, and have we made plain our capacity or otherwise to provide this, and the likely costs or other factors which we shall need to impose?

16. Do we need specific facilities to be made available by the customer at specified times, and is this being made plain?

17. If our system is required to work in the customer's environment as a condition of acceptance, will there be an opportunity to reproduce that environment for intermediate testing, or must everything await final test? What does this do to the risks we may face?

18. Do we need access in advance to the customer's working environment to ensure acceptability before we deliver, and is this being made available to us as of right?

Staff

1. Do we need staff with specific skills, and do we have them available? If not, can we obtain them outside?
2. Shall we have the budget to train them if necessary?
3. Will the project offer suitable experience to motivate our people, or does it represent merely a 'bread and butter' opportunity? If the latter, are we allowing for rotation of staff, wastage, or project terminal bonuses to retain key people, if appropriate?
4. Have individual staff with given profiles of experience been mentioned and/or introduced to the customer? Is there any understanding that they, as individuals, will be made available to the project, or is it understood that suitable substitutes may be provided?

Legal, commercial and financial matters

1. Is the customer contract dependent upon any special funding, from government sources for instance? If so, will our tender be subject to terms or conditions imposed upon the customer and do we know what these are? Will they be acceptable to us?
2. Are we seeking any stage payments? Are we being obliged to secure these by the granting of bank guarantees or other sureties? Do we have access to advice from those who understand such documents, and is this the best route to take anyway?
3. Likewise regarding Letters of Credit and such like? Normally such devices are only applicable to export business.
4. What provisions do we have against the customer defaulting on his obligations? Would the deliverables be re-assignable to others? Might they have a market value? If an export order, are we requiring cash against documents or some other device to ensure we receive payment against physical shipment? If in UK, what credit check have we made against the customer? How financially stable is he?
5. If this is an overseas order, under whose legal code are we obliged to tender? If not the Law of England and under English courts, what provision are we making for costly overseas dispute resolution, if it is at all likely to arise?
6. Do we have suppliers or sub-contractors upon whom we will be reliant? Is someone reviewing the same checklist upon them as we are upon the prospective customer?
7. Is our proposed price commercially viable, and is it sound?
8. What is the proposed structure of stage payments? Does it match our cash flow, and has a comparison been carried out? Possession being 'nine points of the law', it can be important in bargaining power to have a cash inflow which

matches cash outflow, even though stage payments may be contingent upon ultimate completion.

9. In constructing cash flow, have all retention moneys, commissions and deductions been allowed for?

10. If overseas currencies are involved, have foreign exchange fluctuations been allowed for? Are the sums sufficient to allow for international treasury transactions to be executed to mitigate forex losses?

11. Has the effect of taxation, both in the UK and overseas, been allowed for?

12. Is the customer and any other relevant party financially sound? How do we know? When did we last check?

13. If overseas bank accounts are needed, are the arrangements being put in place? How much will they cost?

14. Is there a warranty period during which faults and/or support has to be provided at no further cost? Has allowance been made for this?

15. Is it clear what we have to deliver, and/or to get accepted, in order to secure payment?

Political and regional factors

1. If execution of the contract takes place abroad, are the regions concerned politically stable?

2. What are living conditions like for expatriates? Can staff come and go without hindrance? Might families accompany the work force, and are there social difficulties if they do?

3. Might there be exchange control problems in obtaining payment and taking it out of the region or country? Are there recognised ways of ensuring payment against delivery or against documents of title, which minimise the risk of legal proceedings to enforce payment in a foreign land and legal code?

4. How about internal communications and transport – for materials as well as people?

5. If secrecy or confidentiality requirements are part of the contract terms, are they reasonable in the circumstances and are they compatible with local law?

6. If we are members of a group of companies, is there local experience or knowledge among associated enterprises which might help us?

7. Are we selling into a territory where local commission agents are compulsory? If so, have we an agent? If we have ever had another one in the past, are we certain that any obligation to him has expired? In some countries agencies persist regardless of any term or termination provision in the written agency agreement. It is sometimes necessary to procure termination, for which a fee might be payable. Failure to do this could involve us in two lots of commission on the same contract. The amount of support given by some of these agents can be immaterial in establishing their right to be paid, and local law will often support them.

8. Is there a British Embassy or Consulate in the territory which might give support? Have we approached the Department of Trade and Industry?

Planning and estimating

1. Have we been given or have we drawn up an explicit and unambiguous statement of the customer's requirements?

2. Is there a project plan, with intermediate milestones or objectives against which progress can be measured?

3. Unless we have a highly developed estimating process, or unless the product is standard, has the project been broken down into elements small enough to enable costing and estimating to be properly carried out?

4. Have we allowed adequate time and money to cover management and administration of the contract?

5. Has a cash flow statement been produced? Does it go 'negative'? When, and by how much? How sensitive is cash flow to milestones being reached or not reached? In what circumstances might stage payments or instalments be delayed, and what effect might that have upon cash receivable?

6. If the project is sufficiently complex, has a PERT[1] or similar means of examining items or similar network been drawn up? If the higher mathematical tools are not available to us, has anyone carried out a simple 'at best', 'at worst', and 'likely' analysis of time and cost, just adding up each column, so that we know overall sensitivities which might impact upon profit or loss on the job?

7. Having identified the sensitive areas, have we decided we must live with them, or can the customer be enlisted to help us off-load our risk? If not the customer, how about a supplier or sub-contractor?

8. Have external events been analysed and allowed for? Site access under the control of third parties? Undertakings of the customer to make available facilities that we shall need and only he can provide? Accommodation that our people will need? Services such as light, heat, power, or even computer services if these are relevant?

9. Is the project plan at the tender phase sufficiently clear for our ultimate project leader to understand it and act upon it, as and when we are awarded the job? If the customer has a part to play in it, does he understand this, and has he confirmed willingness? If so, does he have the right skilled staff or facilities to undertake his obligations?

10. Has the plan been specifically discussed and agreed with the customer?

11. Has a list been constructed of all the testing and other facilities which we shall need? Which of these are not under our control? Have we sought binding undertakings from those who will make them available to us, as a prerequisite to making any undertakings to the customer? (Have we also firm undertakings from any of our colleagues that our *own* facilities will be available to us?)

12. If our estimating procedures are not standardised or highly developed, has a second opinion been sought, perhaps from a colleague with relevant experience but who is independent of the bid team? Much effort and enthusiasm goes into proposals, and it is all too easy for objectivity to suffer.

---

[1] PERT = Programme Evaluation and Review Technique: a mathematical way of reviewing the interaction of time-critical activities on a project to reveal where and how much slack there may be in the schedule, which slippages can become crucial, and at what point. Features the use of 'at best, at worst, and likely' forecasting for each element and in total.

13. In our estimate sheets, is the true estimated cost shown before applying policy or other discounts?

14. Have we allowed adequate contingency allowances in those areas where we have little knowledge or confidence in estimating?

15. Is it clear how many contingency allowances and discounts have been applied *in total*, to avoid accidental double counting?

16. How about inflation, if the contract is to run for any length of time? How about inflation also in overseas territories which may affect us?

17. Have we allowed for travel and subsistence costs? Do they include management visits over the life of the contract?

18. Are there any special requirements regarding security? Have they been allowed for?

Contract clause analysis

1. Is there a 'time of the essence' clause? Is it acceptable to us, possibly because we are entirely confident that the deliverables will be ready in time?

2. If there is no 'time of the essence' clause as such, have we or our agents been made aware that time is in effect essential because of the nature of the customer's situation? If so, the risk may be the same as in (1).

3. Are there any penalty clauses written into the contract? Have we calculated our maximum loss if they are imposed, as well as the 'at best' and the 'likely' outcome? What do we feel are the probabilities of our suffering under any of these clauses, and to what extent? Can we afford it?

4. How are we managing these risks? Is it open to us to insure against any of the occurrences? Can we negotiate a ceiling level above which no further damages are payable? Might we increase the tender price? Might we offer more than one price (a) with the penalties in full and (b) at a lower level with contained risk levels, so that the customer can see what his clauses might cost him?

5. Are there suppliers or sub-contractors whose non-performance or delay could contribute to our difficulties? Can we pass some of the risk down to them?

6. A common avoidance clause is '*It is nonetheless provided that the damages payable hereunder shall not exceed the contract value*' or '*x percent of the contract value*'. Have we considered inserting such a clause?

7. If there are heavy penalties for delay, have we examined the *force majeure* clause to see whether it is wide enough to protect us from delays we cannot control? Does the proposed penalty for delay take account of *force majeure*, or can we renegotiate it so that it does?

8. Are we obliged to reach certain standard or 'benchmark' performance levels, and are we confident we can do so? Are we sure that we know what they are and that they have been allowed for?

9. Are there any indemnity clauses in the contract, whereby we undertake to indemnify the customer for given situations? If so, have these been submitted to our insurance advisers? Are there any insurance clauses as such? These should also be cleared by specialists in that field.

10. Do we perceive any other areas of concern within the contract clauses as such? Foreign legal codes or jurisdictions? Complex arbitration processes? Clauses obliging our personnel to sign undertakings with the customer?

Sub-contractors and suppliers

1. Are items to be procured standard and easily obtainable in the time allowed, or do we have to consider carefully the status and quality of our sub-contractors and suppliers?

2. Are our routine purchase order or other procurement procedures adequate in this case, or should the bid team become directly involved in selection? For instance, are one or more sources of supply sufficiently critical to the success of the project as to be able to place it in jeopardy by failure to deliver or to perform?

3. Do we have past experience of these sources of supply?

4. Is there a choice, or is there a sole source of supply?

5. What do we know about their standard of workmanship and their financial stability?

6. Is their management stable, and is their culture sufficiently compatible with our own to make working relationships straightforward?

7. Are there terms and conditions within an Invitation to Tender to which we are responding, which require compliance in certain respects by our suppliers and sub-contractors? If so, have they been furnished with details and are the prices offered to us based upon their full compliance? Quality standards, for instance? Security? Site access? Compliance with instructions by the ultimate customer? Certificates of insurance? Particular contract clauses?

8. Are there contract clauses which, if copied down in a suitable form to the sub-contractors, would mitigate exposure to risks which otherwise would be overbearing to us? Have we sensibly exploited opportunities in this respect, and in time for any price adjustments from the suppliers? Usually it will be best for liabilities to rest within the enterprise which has the actual power to manage or control them, lest the risk patterns become unduly distorted.

9. Will our standard goods inwards and inspection or acceptance routines be adequate in this instance, or will they have to be modified? Are materials to be delivered direct to site, for instance, and shall we have to arrange for our own site inspection? How much extra will this cost us?

Quality

1. Are there specific quality standards to which we have to be compliant? These may include:

(a) International standards such as ISO 9000 or BS 5750 which have to do with the manner in which we manage our quality programmes.

(b) Technical quality standards, dealing with dimensions, tolerances, shop floor inspection and control.

(c) Programmes such as Total Quality Management (TQM) which have more to do with organisational philosophy, staff attitudes and motivation.

It can be important that we understand the differences, and know which are applicable in our own case. Many customers require adherence to ISO 9000, for instance, as a condition of the tender. Quality control issues may be addressed in the body of technical specification to which by implication we are accepting.

2. Does a Quality Assurance (QA) plan have to be produced, and have we allowed time and cost to cover it?

3. Have we allowed for the time and cost of other QA activities such as Project Reviews, and Quality Audits?

4. Has any staff training required by QA policy been allowed for?

We may feel a questionnaire as long as this is quite inappropriate for our needs. Many questions might be dispensed with. Others more applicable may be introduced.

Some organisations analyse their needs and produce alternative sets of questions for low, medium or high risk situations, or for home as against overseas contracts, or for 'customer specials' as against standard lines. Others may place a value constraint, whereby only those jobs above a certain cost threshold are submitted to the full review process.

Although the size and value of a contract is clearly a major factor in risk analysis, and although managements are rightly concerned about it, some of the questions themselves serve to remind us that size is not the only determinant of risk. Possibly the greatest risks of all arise from contracts with apparently low profiles of danger and size, but which take us into marketing or technical areas where we have not been before. We assume we know the answers, extrapolating from experience in supposedly similar areas, and we discover our mistake when it is all too late. 'Threshold of Technology' contracts are notorious in this respect. Over the last 20 years many large, confident organisations entered the field of computers, incorrectly believing it to be like any other engineering matter. Mistakes of this kind can be costly.

Portfolios of risk

It is in handling the very real uncertainties of commercial life that we can learn from other businesses whose bread and butter lies in balancing risks: those who manage our investments for us. A prime rule in investment is that one spreads one's risks. No one can be certain which of a group of equity stocks are going to outperform the market, so we invest in a basket of them.

No one can be sure whether equities are at the top or at the bottom of a cycle, though there may be many elaborate theories backed up by arithmetic. For this reason many private investors stage their purchases over a period, and unit trust or PEP savings schemes have been developed to make this easy for us.

Another rule is that we do not hazard that which we cannot afford to lose. If we have assets to invest, we shall be advised to keep a sensible proportion of them in cash on deposit, or in interest bearing 'safe' securities against the possibility of a prolonged 'bear market'. In this way we shall not be forced to withdraw from the higher risk areas at a time when we can only do so at maximum loss.

In investment we expect higher reward for accepting higher risk. This might be measured in terms of higher profits or dividends or in likelihood of capital growth.

The profile of asset distribution should match the profile of obligation or liability, including time frames. Hence a new pension fund with many young contributors may hold most of its assets in equities, since it will be many years before pensions become payable and it may feel able to take the view that in the long run equities will do better than gilts. A more mature fund with a great many pensioners, however, might invest most of its assets in gilts – possibly indexed linked – to match its direct obligations. The risk-taking days are over.

In a business enterprise, matters of this kind are normally board matters. In devising a contract risk management programme it is important that the issues are clearly understood at all relevant levels. A company owned by young entrepreneurs with ambition, marketable skills, and time on their side, might decide to adopt a portfolio with a significant proportion of high risk contracts offering the promise of high market growth and reward if all goes well. If the worst happens and they lose all their money, there is time to start again.

A 'blue chip' company with many factories, staff and products, and dominated by institutional pension fund investors who have put their money in for totally different reasons will behave quite differently. It may carry a proportion of hazardous contracts in its business portfolio, but the main lines may be required to conform to conservative levels of risk.

Of course there are exceptions to most rules. The 'blue chip' organisation threatened with obsolescence – and there have been a few of these – may adopt desperate measures to break into new markets for survival. This may mean rewriting many of the risk procedures, at least in respect of the new business ventures.

What this chapter is all about, however, is to help you avoid your organisation adopting high risk liabilities believing them to be low risk, and declining low risk, high reward opportunities because 'the system' mistakenly classifies them as high risk. As Shakespeare put it 'There is a tide in the affairs of men which taken at the flood leads on to fortune . . .'. In present markets the Customer is King, and monarchs are apt to get impatient if kept waiting about. The day after a crucial Invitation to Tender arrives is no time to start thinking about these matters. The company which does not have strategies in place and the processes or procedures to back them up is unlikely to survive.

Summary

1. Managing business risk is not unlike managing personal risk. Think about an area of personal risk management that we may understand well, such as motor insurance, life or pensions, and seek analogies in the business project risks which we meet.

2. Consider insurance whenever it makes sense. Remember:
   (a) Some risks must be insured against by law.
   (b) For some risks the insurance premiums are low in relation to the protection or peace of mind offered.
   (c) Some risks are difficult or expensive to cover. The underwriter is probably as scared of them as we are, and he knows about such matters. Allow time to think about them, and take advice.
   (d) For some risks we have some choice.

3. Consider the size and character of the enterprise, relative to the size of contracts and their risks.

4. Construct contract or project checklists to suit the organisation. Make them as short and simple as you can, consistent with being comprehensive. Aim to cover:
   - The project profile, costs and rewards
   - Sales implications
   - Staff
   - Legal, commercial and financial matters
   - Political and regional factors
   - Planning and estimating
   - Renegotiating risky contract clauses
   - Sub-contractors and suppliers
   - Quality.

5. Bearing in mind the size of the company, consider the contract risks as if they were a portfolio of investments:
   (a) Spread the risks over a 'basket' of contracts.
   (b) Do not engage in many high risk contracts all at the same time.
   (c) Do not hazard more than the company can afford to lose.
   (d) Seek higher reward for higher risk.

6. Consider what performance profile the company and its owners expect, then:
   (a) Allocate 'desired' proportions or percentages to high, medium and low risk areas.
   (b) Accept that the market is unlikely to deliver opportunities just like that, and affix variance levels that the management can live with.
   (c) Keep a running total in the register of active contracts to monitor compliance with those levels of risk. Inform management at regular intervals, and whenever the tolerances are about to be breached.

7

Techniques of negotiating

An essential aspect of contracts management is the ability to negotiate. Negotiation is not so much a technique as a 'life skill'. Everyone learns ways to negotiate from a very early age. Some of these ways are successful in business life; some are not. Many of us tend to use methods with which we feel comfortable, even though these may not be the best methods in every case.

Much research has been carried out over the years into the techniques of negotiation. Many good books have been written on the subject. One of these, *Getting to Yes* (Fisher and Ury, 1982) is based upon the findings of the Harvard Law School Negotiation Project. Some of the techniques it describes were used with success in the Camp David political talks on the Middle East which took place in 1978. If this seems a long time ago, it may be well to remind ourselves that in negotiating, as in many other subjects, there is little that has not been tried and tested at some time in the past. The secret lies in assimilating that which works, and translating it into a plan of action which we can understand, accept and implement within our own particular organisation today.

The underlying theory behind the Harvard approach is that principled negotiation works best. The party to a negotiation who plays unprincipled tricks to get his way may 'win', as it were, in a single contest where the parties never meet again. Most business deals are not like that. A continuing relationship of some kind is almost certain to result. In such an environment the player of dirty tricks will live to have others played against him by way of retaliation. In these cases not only does that party lose, but the whole relationship loses. Reasons for negotiating in accordance with principle include the following:

(a) Lasting business relationships are built upon trust.

(b) It is easier to be consistent when one is dealing honestly.

(c) Most negotiators perform better against principles to which they can relate.

(d) It is easier than one might think to make the unprincipled bargainer feel uncomfortable and ultimately to give way.

(e) 'In a good bargain, everybody benefits'. These are the contracts that tend to work. With bad bargains, whatever the agreement may have been at the time, those who later feel victimised are likely to be untiring in their efforts to find loopholes.

In practical terms, the aim is to separate the people from the task of getting agreement itself, so that negotiators from each side become solvers of the common problem rather than adversaries. The desired outcome is an agreement which is sound and satisfactory to all, rather than 'A's position' as against 'B's position'.

Another tenet is to avoid taking fixed positions at the outset, such as 'we will not settle for a penny less than £x.' There may indeed be circumstances where at the end of the day we will want to do just that. So we start by exploring all possibilities without commitment. What are our own interests? What are those of the other party? How many of these are common to both? How many more could, with some adjustment, become common interests? Are there any other areas – right outside the immediate scope of the negotiation – where the parties have common goals that could with profit be brought into the discussions?

What are the true conflicts of interest between us? Before we begin to fall out over them, are there constructive ways of mitigating the effects of these conflicts?

Seek to establish objective criteria which can be applied to each proposition. Test the proposals against those objects. What is the underlying principle behind each argument? Try only to yield to principled arguments, not those based upon pressure.

Preparing to negotiate

A key message behind the Harvard Law School approach, and perhaps the most important single one to remember in a company environment, is the importance of *preparation*. Before a negotiation ever starts we should have completed a checklist. This might include the following items:

─────────────────────── **Checklist** ───────────────────────

Ourselves

1. What are our objectives: what do we want to achieve from the negotiation?

2. What are our strong points? And our weaknesses?

3. What objectives do we have in common with the other party? How can we use them in negotiation?

4. Which of our objectives are likely to be in conflict? Can we think of ways to mitigate the effect of these?

5. What are our alternatives if we totally fail to reach agreement? (the Harvard text calls this our 'Best Alternative to a Negotiated Settlement', or BATNA). The better our BATNA is, the stronger our bargaining position. We might spend time considering alternative BATNA's, or trying to improve upon the ones we have.

6. When negotiations start, what is our 'trip wire' to be? A 'trip wire' is a position better than one equal to our BATNA, but which is sufficiently unfavourable for us to wish to break off discussions while we think. It can be important to have this established in advance. Negotiating teams tend to get committed to the deals they are working on, and it can be tempting after an arduous series of talks to concede 'just one more concession to get us a deal'. This temptation should be resisted, and the fixing of an arbitrary 'trip wire' can be a good way of doing so.

The other party

7. It is now necessary to answer all the same questions as we perceive the other party would do so for himself. What are his interests and conflicts? His BATNA? His 'trip wire'?

8. What does this tell us about the way we should be conducting negotiations?

Our team

9. Who is going to do what?

10. When?

11. How large should it be?

12. Who shall lead it, and what parts will other members play?

Negotiating tactics

In many respects the Harvard Law School approach to negotiating represents the strategic approach to the subject. Yet every negotiation is to some extent at the mercy of the shrewd tactician, and it is important to be aware of the tactics one may meet, how to recognise them, how to play them ourselves when it seems appropriate, and what the antidotes may be when we find them being played against us.

There are many books and learning cassettes on the market which deal with negotiating tactics. A number of the author's favourites are listed at the back of this book. In his experience, however, the one negotiating tactic which is most talked about but least often practised is to BE PREPARED.

Preparation involves more than one aspect. To begin with, are we familiar with the area of negotiating we are about to enter or is it new ground? Does it call for technical expertise, or merely 'savvy' and the gift of recognising a good deal when one sees it? To take a simple example, few of us would consider buying a used car without at least consulting Parker's Guide. If we could not get hold of a copy, we might be wise to defer our car buying until we could. Better still, we might talk to or enlist the support of a local motor engineer to advise us on price strategy, and even to take a look under the bonnet for us. If none of these options were open to us, we might decide to buy from a recognised dealer of repute, backed by such extended warranty as we could secure. This could cost us a little more, since dealers are known to be some of the most skilled negotiators in the business.

Alternatively, we might elect to take an entirely empirical route, and seek to buy from a neighbour, or someone within our own district who might be less likely to sell us short. In such cases we would be looking less at the mechanics (about which we may know little) and more at the income bracket of the seller, the service history of the car, what manner of person had driven it, and the ascertainable reason for selling. A story was told many years ago of an army colonel who made an excellent purchase in this way. How could he be so sure, someone asked him? 'Well', he replied, 'I noticed that in addition to everything else being in good order, the owner took the trouble to have the interior wind up clock to the exact time, even though he did not know I was coming. I figured that anyone who took that good care of his vehicle had probably looked after the servicing well too.' Most of us can recall instances of sound purchases made in this way, and often they are less empirical judgements than they may have seemed.

To emphasise the importance of preparation, however, and the stress that we lay upon it, here are some planning charts to help you ensure that your organisation has thought about negotiating, about what is needed, about which kind of people are required, about who is available, and about how to use them.

Background Information – Preparing to Negotiate

What are the kinds of negotiation our organisation is likely to engage in?

What background information is needed to recognise a 'good deal' from an indifferent one?

       Sales catalogues
       Market surveys
       Financial Times reports
       Others

How much of that information is presently available?

How long will it take to assemble any background data which is not immediately to hand?

How important is it?

    Until such questions have been addressed, we are not ready to negotiate

---

Subject of Negotiation

Purpose of Negotiation:

Acquisition or sale of goods?
Acquisition or sale of services?
A 'one-off' deal?
A long standing business relationship?
Other?

Criteria for success:

Lowest price?
Highest price (to sell)?
Quantity?
Quality?
Consistency?
Flexibility of relationship?
Other?

Background or reference material required:

Qualities of Team Members

What experience does this team member have of negotiating?

What negotiating experience in *this class of deal*?

What personality traits are ascribed to this member?

> Introvert
> Extrovert
> 'Hard'
> 'Soft'
> Other attributes which may either help or hinder relationships

In which role is team member perceived as being most effective in this instance?

> Team leader
> Specialist (engineer, salesman, accountant, estimator)
> Contract or legal draftsman
> Observer and recorder (role being to observe passively, to note behaviour of opposing team, and to be prepared to analyse psychological or other factors and to be ready to report to and advise team leader as a result)

Other relevant character or personality traits

Roles of Members During Negotiation

Who will be Team Leader? How will the role be performed? (This may be pro-actively, by clearly co-ordinating the discussions and controlling other team members. Alternatively, the Team Leader might take a background role, saying very little, observing a lot, taking discreet notes and controlling final developments through another extrovert member of the team.)

Which team members will undertake specialist areas?

> Engineering
> Costing or estimating
> Legal interpretation
> Drafting or re-drafting

Who will take note of decisions reached, concessions made or won? How will any drafting or re-drafting of documents be conducted? If possible, retain control of this process especially when negotiating away from home.

Who will make key decisions to settle, withdraw to confer, or to break off negotiations altogether? How will this be communicated to the team and/or to the other side? How will individual team members indicate their wish to pause for a review, without necessarily revealing their position to the other side?

Are there any other key 'signals' which should be agreed between the team members before the negotiation commences? Are such signals clearly understood?

Perceptions of Opposing Team

Who is the perceived Team Leader?

What are the roles of the other members?

What personality types are they?

      Introvert
      Extrovert
      'Hard'
      'Soft'
      Other Characteristics

Where does the authority lie?

      With the Team Leader?
      With someone else in the Team?
      Perhaps with the silent member who says little?
      Outside the Team altogether?

The telephone negotiation

Consider the telephone negotiation – one of the most dangerous business devices of today. Have some defence mechanisms ready.

1.   For the recipient of the call: 'I'm in a meeting. What is the subject?' Listen carefully and *do not speak*. Then say 'I'll ring you back'. Get prepared and do so.
2.   For the caller: 'I need to speak to you now because we have a special offer.' Explain it briefly. Say 'It is exceptional value, but I need a decision now because [my supplier won't wait] [the market is rising/falling] [any other reason that is

---

plausible].' The really well prepared telephone seller will have a tried and tested script on the desk, possibly in algorithmic form, with considered responses for each version of 'no' which he is likely to get from the other side.

3. Problems with telephone negotiations: lack of warning; insufficient documentation ('where is that file?'); interruptions from colleagues.

4. Opportunities when you are the caller: lay out material first; choose the time to suit you; have a script, which will force you to consider objectives, BATNA, trigger points, and such like. Position yourself where no one can interrupt you.

5. Remember the power of time in telephoning. People feel they have to be brief because of the cost of the call. Consequently a prolonged silence from you can produce tension. It may induce the other party to break silence and give information or make concessions just to reduce the tension. This can work regardless of whose telephone account is at stake, simply because of 'telephone culture'.

6. Always have near any telephone you use: paper, pen or pencil, calculator.

7. Keep notes of the telephone call and, as already stated, confirm in writing.

8. It can often be advantageous to be the party to summarise the call before ringing off: 'Let us just get this clear, we have agreed X and you have agreed Y. OK?'

The 'back burner'

In many negotiations one party will take a printed contract from the other, and will comment aggressively on each clause, demonstrating how it is unreasonable or inapplicable in this particular case, and will call for a concession. It may be that the other side feels impelled to give way, for one reason or another, and is tempted to say so. The problem here is that the aggressive party may follow up with a string of these 'reasonable' situations, progressively winning a series of minor concessions which in total add up to a very unsatisfactory deal indeed for the party which has conceded.

The gambit here is never to concede on the spot. The most one says is that the point is noted, the request is recorded, and when all other discussions are completed, the request will be taken into account. For the time being, the subject remains on the 'back burner' as it were, while other issues are being addressed.

The first time a defending negotiator takes this attitude there may be resentment. By the second or third instance, not only will it be realised that he really means it, but it will become apparent to everyone present that it was the only sensible line he could take. In effect, the other side have been rumbled!

Conclusion.   At the outset we stated that negotiating is a life skill. One goes on learning as long as one lives. The thoughts and ideas in this chapter are merely a beginning. The serious negotiator will follow up all the literature on the subject, and above all will *practise* negotiating.

The single most important step to take is *preparation*. Before a negotiation ever starts, know what you want and whether it is realistic. To conclude, here is the final planning sheet, based on the Harvard Law School approach.

Negotiation planning sheet

Our aims:	Their perceived aims:
Our interests:	Their perceived interests:
What we have to lose:	What we think they have to lose:

Interests in common:

Our BATNAs[1] (list them all and choose the best)	What their BATNAs are likely to be:
Our 'trip wire':	Their likely 'trip wire':
Our people: how the team will work:	Who will be in their team; how are they likely to work together:

[1]BATNA: The Best Alternative to a Negotiated Settlement. In simple terms, what we will do if the talks break down and we never reach agreement. The better our BATNA, the better we shall feel!

Summary

1. Negotiating is a life skill. We keep on learning better techniques through-out our lives.
2. Lasting relationships are built on trust and principle. Only the 'quick deal' may benefit from sharp practice.
3. The most effective single step in negotiating is to *prepare* for it; it is often the most neglected step.
4. Learn to use time in negotiating. It can be powerful if you have it, devastating if you do not.
5. Take it slowly. Beware of the quick deal.
6. Learn 'cockpit drill' for the telephone negotiation. Always have the equipment to hand, or else delay taking the call.
7. The toughest opposition in negotiating may come not from the counter-party but from our own organisation. Take time to get to know it, and how to work with it so that it works with you. If that means massaging corporate egos, so be it!
8. Remember the other side have egos too.
9. Try to be the side that drafts the contract or other document. This gives power, like the player who serves in tennis.
10. Better still, have a printed contract that no one has the authority to alter! The 'ace serve' as it were.
11. 'Walking out' of talks can be a valuable weapon. Be prepared to use it, and do not be overwhelmed if the other side uses it against you. It does not have to be final.
12. If you forget most of these ideas, try to recall one tenet at least: BE PREPARED!

8

Sales of goods and services; outsourcing

Sales of goods and services

Sales of goods are governed in the main by the Sale of Goods Act 1979. This has since been amended by the Sale of Goods and Services Act 1982, which also covers services. The law has been further amended by the Sale and Supply of Goods Act 1994 which came into force on 3 January 1995. This latest Act contains clauses amending all of the other Acts in various respects, though it may be a few years before cases emerge which test and clarify the exact effects of this latest Act. So what are the key points that contract staff need to know about the selling of goods and services in a commercial situation?

Let us first examine sales of goods.

Sales of goods

Sales of goods involve the transfer of goods in return for money. Goods may be sold by simple contract, the rules for which have been defined elsewhere. So what are goods?

Goods are defined as all personal chattels apart from money and 'choses in action'. Personal chattels are movable things, and they may include animate creatures such as horses as well as inanimate objects. Those objects must not be connected with land. Real estate (land and buildings) are not goods, nor are items of intellectual property. Choses in action are items that we can only obtain after pursuing a successful court action to recover them. Those are not classed as 'goods' until we have actually recovered them. Growing trees are not classed as goods, but felled timber is.

Consideration for the sale of goods must include at least some money, otherwise it is a barter. A key aspect to the sale of goods is that there should be a *delivery*. If there are no deliverables, pause and consider whether it is in fact an item of goods which is being sold. (Beware, however, that the converse is not always true; just because there are deliverables it doesn't necessarily mean that goods are an essential feature of the contract.)

Goods may be in existence at the time of the sale, or else they may be contemplated; sales of goods 'off the drawing board'. When the goods are transferred across at the time of making the contract, the agreement is classed as a sale. When transfer is to happen later, it is said to be an 'agreement to sell'. A contract to hire goods is not a sale of goods under the Act – this falls under the Supply of Goods and Services Act 1982.

The price for the goods may be fixed by the contract, or else it may be decided in the course of dealing between the parties. If the matter is left open, then the buyer has to pay a reasonable price, however that may be determined by the court.

We have elsewhere discussed the difference between 'conditions' which are essential parts of the contract, and 'warranties' which are binding in themselves but ancillary matters. If the seller breaches a condition then the buyer may:

1. Treat the contract as irrevocably broken, return the goods (or make them available for collection) and demand return of any money paid. He may also claim damages, or
2. Keep the goods and sue for damages.

If the buyer has already accepted some or all of the goods, then he only has the 'damages' remedy unless the contract stipulates otherwise. Typically this might happen in a 'time the essence' contract where the items are useless to the buyer unless he has all of them by a certain known date.

It is important to understand the rules on time. Time of delivery is as often as not a condition, striking at the root of the agreement. Time of payment, unless otherwise stated, is just a warranty. Payment itself is, of course, a condition.

Implied terms in sales of goods

Several key conditions and warranties are implied by statute in sales of goods. This means that they will apply unless in certain circumstances they are expressly excluded. What are these terms?

1. *Title.* The seller implies that he owns or has a valid title to the goods enabling him to sell. If he does not, he will be liable in damages. In 'agreements to sell' it may be sufficient if that title exists at the time the goods pass, so that agreements to sell items which the seller later buys from the manufacturer will be quite valid, other things being equal.
2. *Description.* The goods must match the description given. If the buyer has been shown a sample, then the goods must match both the description and the sample.
3. *Satisfactory quality.* When the seller is a business and not selling in a private capacity, the goods must be of 'satisfactory quality'. The 1994 Act introduced this term to replace the more archaic 'merchantable quality'. 'Satisfactory quality' is further defined as meeting 'the standard that a reasonable person would regard as satisfactory, taking account of any description of the goods, the price (if relevant) and all other relevant circumstances'.
4. *Fitness for purpose.* Once again this applies to business sellers. The goods must be fit for their purpose, which the 1994 Act clarifies as:
(a) fit for all the purposes for which goods of the kind in question are commonly supplied;

(b) as regards appearance and finish;
(c) as regards freedom from minor defects;
(d) safety;
(e) durability.

The seller, however, does have an escape from all this to the extent of:

(f) any matters which were brought to the buyer's attention before the contract was made;
(g) if the buyer examined the goods before purchase, then any matters which examination ought to have revealed;
(h) if the buyer bought by sample, then any matters which examination of the sample ought to have revealed.

5.   *Regarding samples*. When it is agreed that the buyer buys from a sample, then the bulk of the goods must correspond with the quality of the sample. The buyer must be given a reasonable chance to compare the bulk with the sample, and the goods must be free from any material defect which reasonable examination of the sample would not have revealed. As in so much of English mercantile law, the test here is 'what is reasonable?'.

Unfair contract terms

The law in general states that implied terms can be overridden by express clauses. The Unfair Contract Terms Act of 1977, however, restricts some of this freedom by statute. (For consumer contracts the Unfair Terms in Consumer Contracts Regulations 1994 have additionally applied since July 1995, implementing the Unfair Terms Directive of the EU. As few business contracts are concerned with the individual consumer, the Regulations are not considered here in depth; a brief summary is given later in this chapter.) The key provisions of the 1977 Act, which deals with exclusion clauses, are these. No party which is contracting in a business capacity may:

1.   Exclude unlimited liability for damages due to death or injury to third parties, arising from the contracting party's negligence.
2.   Exclude liability for any other loss or damage, save and to the extent that it is fair and reasonable in the circumstances which were known, contemplated, or ought to have been known or contemplated at the time the contract was made.

Furthermore, the courts will take into account the following factors in deciding what was 'reasonable':

1.   The relative bargaining strengths of the parties, taking into account such aspects as 'single source suppliers'.
2.   Whether the buyer received any inducement to accept the exclusion clause, once again taking into account any alternative sources he may or may not have had, and the conditions laid down by those sources.
3.   Whether the customer knew, or ought reasonably to have known, of the clause.

4. Whether, if the exclusion clause was triggered by the buyer breaching some condition of the contract, compliance with that condition was considered reasonably practicable at the time of the contract.
5. Whether or not the goods were standard or made to order.

One ancillary test of reasonableness is whether, and to what extent, the buyer might have protected himself by insurance from the excluded risk, and whether it was reasonable to have expected this. Some authorities hold that since evidence of bargaining for 'special deals' might help the seller claim that some exclusions were reasonable, a well thumbed and amended sale contract might be advantageous rather than a standard unaltered printed set of terms.

A further point is that clauses *limiting* rather than *excluding* liability are less likely to be harshly treated under the Act.

Special care needs to be taken by sellers who in the course of business deal with buyers who 'deal as consumers'. A party deals as a consumer when the goods he is buying are of a kind normally provided for private use and the buyer is not buying or holding himself out as buying in a business capacity. In such cases the courts will interpret the law strictly against the seller, and most of the implied terms will operate against the buyer whether or not they have been expressly excluded.

Where consumers are buying the courts are particularly harsh against exclusion clauses which come to the attention of the buyer after the making of the contract. This may happen where standard terms are not declared at the time but are displayed in places where the buyer would go only after the sale had been made, such as in an hotel bedroom. The reception desk is the point at which the agreement is established. (Once again, see the section later in this chapter dealing with the Unfair Contract Terms in Consumer Contracts Regulations.)

Transfer of property

It can be important to know the exact point at which ownership of goods passes from buyer to seller. This may be because of the need to insure, to decide who suffers if the items are lost, stolen or damaged, or in the case of insolvency of either party, who does and does not have the right of possession or repossession.

1. Specific goods pass at the time the parties intend it to pass. That much is easy. In the absence of any specific intention, however, the following rules apply:
(a) If the goods are in a deliverable state, ownership passes as soon as the contract is made.
(b) If there is work to be dome first, the goods pass when the work has been done and the buyer has been told.
(c) Where there is some measuring, testing or quality control to be done by the seller, then that has to be done first and the buyer told.
(d) In the case of goods on sale or return or on approval, ownership passes:
  (i) When the buyer indicates approval, expressed or implied, or
  (ii) When the buyer keeps the goods beyond a stated time, or in the absence of that, beyond a reasonable time, without having signified rejection.

2. Different rules apply to unascertained goods such as 'one ton of coal' out of a supply depot which may contain 1000 tons. In this case ownership will pass when the goods have been unconditionally allocated to the buyer's contract. This can be done by the seller with the buyer's consent, or by the buyer with the seller's consent. The buyer's agreement may be expressed or implied and may be given before or after the allocation is made.

Transfer of risk

Where the contract is silent, the risk of looking after the goods and suffering loss if they perish passes from seller to buyer at the same time as the passing of the ownership. This may happen whether or not delivery has been made. If delivery is held up through the fault of either party, then the risk will lie with whichever party is at fault.

In practice there may be contract clauses which will greatly vary these provisions. Title and risk may pass either at the same time or at widely differing times if the parties so agree.

What constitutes delivery?

'Delivery' does not imply transport of the goods. It may take place anywhere and in any manner that may be agreed. It may be implied or construed by the acts of the parties, such as the passing of a set of ignition keys to a motor car, or a set of shipping documents in the case of freight. Where they have not expressly agreed, however, the following rules apply:

1. Delivery happens at the seller's place of business. If he has not got one, then it happens at his home.

2. Where the seller is to deliver, it must be within a reasonable period and at a reasonable time.

3. If the goods are being held by a third party, then delivery happens when that party informs the buyer that he now holds the goods on that buyer's behalf.

4. When the seller is authorised to arrange carriage, *prima facie* delivery happens when the goods pass to a carrier, whether or not the buyer has authorised that particular carrier. However, the seller must have made a reasonable contract with the carrier. When sea transit is involved, notice must have been given to the buyer to enable him to arrange insurance, otherwise the risk stays with the seller.

5. If the seller agrees to carry the goods to a place other than the point of sale, then in the absence of any agreement on the matter they go at the buyer's risk. Moreover if, without any negligence, the seller hands them over, by agreement, at the buyer's location to someone having ostensible authority to receive them for the buyer, then risk passes to the buyer at that point.

6. If the seller is ready and willing to deliver and the buyer declines or is unable to accept delivery within a reasonable time, he is liable to the seller for any damages or expenses. This situation may typically arise where site preparation is required to a high standard before sensitive technical equipment may be received and installed. Such agreements need to be carefully worded.

Acceptance

When does acceptance occur? Frequently in technical supply contracts there will be detailed procedures for commissioning and acceptance tests. Subject to any of these, acceptance takes place when the buyer

1.   tells the seller that he has accepted the goods;
2.   does anything to the goods which is inconsistent with the seller continuing to own them, or
3.   retains them beyond a reasonable period without indicating to the seller that he has rejected them.

Where the goods are delivered and the buyer has not previously had a chance to examine them, he must be given a reasonable opportunity to do so. Unless it is a severable contract, if the buyer accepts part of the consignment he loses any right to reject and to claim breach of condition. This does not prevent him from rejecting faulty goods and having them replaced, nor for claiming any damages. What he loses is the right to claim fundamental breach and to repudiate the whole contract. A severable contract is one which is capable of separation.

   This aspect of the law should be carefully remembered by buyers with a 'time of the essence' problem. They should be wary of formally accepting part consignments before they are in a position to receive, examine and accept the whole. They might wish to indicate that acceptance tests have been passed by the early consignments, but it should be made clear that this is without prejudice to their remedy for delay on the whole contract.

   It sometimes happens that with bulk supplies a buyer will send more or less than ordered. It can happen owing to inexactitude of measuring, and may apply not only to bulk but to such items as long print runs where machinery needs time to 'bed down' and exact counting is not appropriate. Unless the contract deals with such matters, however, the buyer may reject all of a 'shorts' or 'overs' consignment. Alternatively he may accept the whole, or merely the amount he ordered and reject the rest. As much as he accepts, so must he pay for at the contract rate.

   The seller may find it convenient to deliver in instalments. Yet unless this has been agreed in the contract, the buyer cannot be compelled to accept part consignments.

What can the seller do if he is unpaid?

Even though title to the goods has passed to the buyer, the seller does have certain remedies if he remains unpaid. They are these:

1.   A lien on the goods, if he still has physical control of them. He can then retain them until he is paid, provided that there was no agreement for credit terms or that, if there were, those arrangements have been broken. He also has a lien if the buyer has become insolvent. He loses the lien, however, at the point where the goods are delivered to a carrier for transmission to the buyer. If property has not yet passed, then he has the right to retain ownership until paid.

2.   If the buyer becomes insolvent, then the seller has an extra remedy. If at that time the goods are still in transit, he may repossess them. 'Insolvency' in this case means failing to meet debts as they fall due. The buyer does not have to have committed one of the formal acts of bankruptcy. Moreover, these rights are in most cases effective against any third party to whom the buyer might have 'sold on'.

3.   In the following cases the seller has the right to resell the goods over which he has control:

(a) if they are perishable goods;
(b) when he has given due notice to the buyer, and the buyer still has not paid; or
(c) where the contract expressly gives him that right.

4.   When property has passed to the buyer, the seller has the right to sue for the price.

5.   When property has not passed, he has that right when the buyer declines or delays acceptance. As with all contract matters, the damages will be the amount actually suffered by the seller. Hence it may be greater with special purpose items than with resaleable standard products.

What are the buyers' rights?

The buyer has the following rights:

1.   He can sue the seller for wrongfully refusing or neglecting to deliver. Damages will be the amount actually suffered.

2.   If he has paid the price, he may sue for recovery.

3.   He may sue for specific performance, but only in those cases where the court considers it to be a proper and necessary remedy – for instance, because the goods are unique. For this remedy to apply the goods themselves must be specific or ascertained.

4.   If a condition has been broken, he may choose *either* to treat the contract as broken, return the goods if he has them, and sue for damages, *or* to regard the breach as a mere breach of warranty.

5.   For a breach of warranty, the buyer may not return the goods but he may sue for damages or have the price amended to reflect the lost value.

Trade descriptions

The Trade Descriptions Acts of 1968 and 1972 create three main criminal offences for misrepresentations about goods. These Acts do not provide civil remedies as such; they are a deterrent to unfair practices. It is an offence to:

1.   Apply a false description to goods or supplies or offers to supply goods to which a false description has been given. 'False' here means false to a material extent, and there is a detailed clause in the Act clarifying the extent of what constitutes 'description'.

2.   Make misleading statements about the price. Typically this refers to 'sales', 'special offers' of a kind which may be less than genuine.

3. Make false statements about services or accommodation. Here the law is addressing 'closing down sales' where the store does not actually close.

The law relating to services

The Supply of Goods and Services Act of 1982 brings some statutory control into a wider spectrum of contract than previously covered by the Sale of Goods Act. Its scope also covers

1. barter or exchange contracts, which were previously excluded because of the lack of money in the price,
2. repair contracts, and
3. contracts for the supply of services as such.

The implied terms here are as to (i) freedom from encumbrances and quiet possession, (ii) description, (iii) satisfactory quality and fitness for purpose, and (iv) sample. In the case of services, there is an implied term that the provider will use reasonable care and skill, within a reasonable time if none is stated, and for a reasonable price where none has been agreed.

Unfair contract terms for consumers, as from 1 July 1995

As a result of a European Union directive, the UK was required to introduce new legislation to help protect individual consumers from terms applied by suppliers to businesses. This new legislation, contained in the Unfair Terms in Consumer Contracts Regulations 1994 (S.I. 1994/No 3159), became effective on 1 July 1995. It applies to contracts between a commercial supplier and an individual consumer, not as between two commercial organisations.

The legislation provides that 'unfair' contract terms shall not be binding upon the consumer, and it specifies that a term is unfair if, contrary to the requirement of 'good faith', it causes a significant imbalance in the parties' rights to the detriment of the consumer. It contains schedules of those matters which may be deemed 'unfair' and of those factors to be applied in assessing 'good faith'.

The legislation does *not* apply to:

- employment contracts;
- contracts relating to succession rights;
- contracts relating to rights under family law;
- contracts relating to company formation or the forming of partnerships; or
- any term incorporated to comply with statutory or regulatory provisions of UK law, or to comply with the principles or provisions of international conventions to which EU countries or the EU itself are committed

It *does* apply to:
- contracts where one party is an individual and the other parties are insurance undertakings, banks and many other categories, though it does not cover those parts of an insurance contract which delimit the insured risk.

All terms *not individually negotiated* between supplier and consumer are subject to this legislation, and are subject to the test of *'unfairness'*. All relevant circumstances will be taken into account. The following non-exhaustive list of terms is scheduled to indicate and provide examples of what might be considered 'unfair' (this is a simplified summary; be sure to have the full text of Statutory Instrument S.I. 3159 available for detailed reference).

Terms which might be 'unfair'

- excluding the legal liability of the supplier arising from *injury or death* to the consumer arising from the supplier's act or omission;
- inappropriately *excluding the legal rights of the consumer* in the event of total or partial non-performance, or inadequate performance. This includes *restriction of the consumer's right to set-off* a debt owed against a payment due;
- making an agreement *binding against the consumer*, whereas provision of *services by the supplier may be voluntary*;
- allowing the *seller* to retain sums paid by the consumer *in the event that the consumer cancels* or does not proceed, *without* a reciprocal right for the *consumer* to recover equivalent compensation *where the seller is the party electing to cancel* or not proceed;
- requiring a *consumer who is in default* to pay a *disproportionately high compensation*;
- *authorising the seller to dissolve* the contract at his discretion *without a reciprocal right* for the consumer;
- allowing the seller to *retain sums paid* where it is *he who has elected to dissolve* the contract;
- *enabling the seller to terminate* a contract of indeterminate length *without reasonable notice*, except where there are serious grounds for doing so. (It is without hindrance, however, to specified financial services contracts, and does not apply to specified stock exchange and foreign exchange linked situations);
- *automatically extending* a contract of fixed length when the consumer remains silent beyond an *unreasonably short fixed deadline* for him or her to indicate intentions;
- *irrevocably binding the consumer* to *terms he had no real chance of examining* before he entered into the contract (but there are modifications to this example where rates of interest and charges in financial services contracts are concerned, or where the consumer is given a corresponding right to dissolve the contract);
- *allowing the seller to alter terms unilaterally* without a valid and stated reason. (It is without hindrance, however, to specified financial services contracts including those involving interest rate changes, and it does not apply to specified stock exchange and foreign exchange linked situations);
- *allowing the seller unilaterally to alter the specification* of the produce or service without a valid reason;
- *allowing the price to be fixed at the time of delivery*, or *allowing the seller to increase the price, without in each case giving the consumer the right to cancel* if the resultant price is too high in relation to the price agreed when

the contract was made (it does not apply to specified stock exchange and foreign exchange linked situations, and is without hindrance to specified price indexation clauses, provided they are lawful and explicitly described);

- *giving the supplier the right to decide* whether or not *the supplies are in accordance with the contract*, or giving him *the exclusive right to interpret a given term*;
- *limiting the seller's obligation to respect commitments made by his agents*;
- *obliging the consumer to perform* all his obligations *where the supplier does not* perform his;
- giving the seller *the right to transfer his obligations* without the consumer's agreement, where that might serve to *reduce the consumer's guarantees*;
- *excluding or hindering the consumers' rights to take legal action*, in various specified ways.

And now for 'good faith'. In assessing whether 'good faith' has been demonstrated, regard shall be had to the following:

Tests of 'good faith'

- The *strengths* of the parties' *bargaining powers*;
- whether the consumer had *an incentive to agree*;
- whether the items were supplied to *the special order of the consumer*;
- the extent to which the supplier has dealt *fairly and equitably* with the consumer.

Rules about 'individually negotiated terms'

A term will always be regarded as *not* individually negotiated where it has been drafted in advance and the consumer has not been able to influence its substance. Where part of the contract has been individually negotiated and part has not, the regulations will continue to be applied to *the part of the contract which has not been individually negotiated*. Moreover, in establishing that individual negotiation has taken place, the burden of proof lies with the supplier.

An incentive to 'keep it simple'

Inherent in the regulations is an incentive to keep the language simple. Regulation 3(2) indicates that '*in so far as it is in plain, intelligible language*', no assessment of fairness will be made of a term which defines the main subject matter or deals with the adequacy of the price. Regulation 6 further specifies that '*the supplier shall ensure that any written term is in plain, intelligible language*', and that '*if there is any doubt* [about the meaning] *the interpretation most favourable to the consumer will prevail*'.

Hence we may expect to see terms such as *mutatis mutandis*, *prima facie*, and long legalistic sentences disappear from the small print that we may come across in the High Street.

What if the terms are considered unfair?

If a term is considered unfair then it will not be binding upon the consumer. He or she may ignore it, thus leaving the other party to sue if it wishes to. There is in addition a procedure whereby the consumer can approach the Director General of Fair Trading to have the term declared unfair and to have it suppressed. Only if the rest of the contract is capable of separate existence can it remain in being.

Action checklist

1. Check whether any of your products or services are supplied to consumers. If so, you may be affected by this legislation. Be sure to have specialist advice available, especially during the first few years of this legislation when experience is being gained and case law emerging.
2. Redraft all terms into the plainest and most simple language (English or Welsh, as appropriate) consistent with preservation of meaning. Most 'readability indices' award good marks for shortness of sentences, and words with few syllables. The problem is that, in English, words with Anglo-Saxon roots are short and ideal for the purpose, but the Latin derived words, though longer, can contain greater depth or precision of meaning. A sensible balance may have to be struck. Ask someone with no university degree and no legal training to examine your draft contracts and to tell you what they think they mean.
3. Consider whether any terms could be considered unfair. Consider how to make them fair – possibly by 'pricing them up', and offering the 'unfair' alternative as a bargain or cut price choice.

Other aspects of law

The law relating to unsolicited goods establishes that in most cases anyone receiving unasked for goods 'out of the blue' as it were, may elect to treat them as a gift. This he may do if the sender either fails to collect within six months, or within one month if called upon to do so in writing. There is specific legislation covering fair trading, consumer safety, and environmental protection.

Outsourcing

In recent years the term 'outsourcing' has been used to describe a series of special relationships which have been established between users of specialised equipment or services, and certain providers of those services. In the early years of outsourcing, most of the instances involved computer or information technology services. This is probably still true in the majority of cases, though like every good idea it now tends to arise in other business situations, where the term has been borrowed.

What is outsourcing

Without delving too deeply into computer industry history, it should be said that it all began in the 1970s under the name 'facilities management'. Typically a company in a business quite unrelated to computers would nonetheless acquire a computer. The company might initially have used the computer to handle something quite mundane such as the payroll, while at the same time recruiting and developing in-house staff with a knowledge of information technology. It was the considered wisdom of those times that to be behind in the race to acquire computer knowledge spelled long-term decline and obsolescence, almost regardless in some cases of the short-term justifications or cost/benefit calculations.

Before long use of the computer would typically be developed further. Sales ledger, bought ledger, other accounting and costing records might be introduced, and even manufacturing management, to the extent that ultimately the entire organisation became heavily dependent upon the computer department, the suppliers of hardware and software, the specialised and highly paid staff who knew how to run the system, and possibly the computer manager himself who – naturally – would have been a product of his own specialised industry.

A problem in management

Yet the company's core business might have nothing to do with computers at all. The company could be a widget manufacturer, a supermarket chain, or even a local authority or a life assurance company. Not only would there be difficulties of culture and understanding – not to mention salary scales – but also a problem that the key computer staff needed to progress their careers by moving to other organisations, like journeymen seeking always the latest techniques to retain their marketability.

The computer systems or software house

The only organisations which could command these people's respect and retain their services were the computer software or systems houses. Such companies would provide support to a variety of clients using many different computer hardware models and software. Job rotation and progression could easily be offered to the brightest candidates, leaving the internal user departments with such talent as was left.

Initially these specialist houses would contract to provide hardware, write and install software, and help to get the system running. Then they might retire, leaving the client to manage his own systems, though some would undertake maintenance and other support for a given scale of fees.

The next step in marketing was to offer facilities management contracts. These might involve systems house staff being seconded to work on the customer's premises full time, operating his computer system for him.

As the service developed further, contracts were written whereby the systems house took over part of the user's records and software and operated them upon the systems houses' sites and hardware. Still further developments resulted in the user purchasing the hardware, software and systems, having them installed at the systems house location and having that systems house maintain and run the systems under contract. The growth of high-quality, high-speed telecommunications links has made the transfer of data from and to the user's location relatively easy, thus freeing him from the risks and complexity of managing his own computer systems.

The arrival of outsourcing

Outsourcing agreements tend to take this process a step or two further. Against a tariff of fees and other charges, the specialist house will take over the hardware, systems, licensed and internally written software and *even the specialised staff* of the computer user. Typically such contracts are of relatively long duration.

Five to ten years' duration is not unknown, and the processes of negotiation and agreement can be intricate. Transfer of staff contracts will be involved including such matters as pension entitlements. Novation of hardware and software agreements will take place with the existing suppliers, entitling the outsourcing organisation to the same facilities and access to intellectual property as the original user. In some instances even transfer of ownership of internal management companies might take place.

The philosophy behind outsourcing is that each organisation does best when focusing upon its core skills. Only computer companies – it is maintained – are truly fitted to run computer systems, and they can do this better and more economically than the user who merely wants his information processed.

At its most highly developed, outsourcing involves close identity and cooperation between the 'outsourcer' and the 'outsourced'. Sometimes each may market products that the other uses. It might be appropriate to have a clause offering incentives or even requiring each to purchase such items only from the other provided that the specifications fit the needs.

Transfer of staff calls for mutual trust of a high order, and much time and effort might be given in the early stages to 'organisational bonding' so that the culture of the one is understood and accepted by the other. This can be one of the more sensitive areas of outsourcing negotiation.

In such an environment it is hardly surprising to find that there are no standard contracts. Each one tends to be individually developed. The most one can do in any discussion of outsourcing is to tabulate some of the items which might need treatment in any agreement that may be reached.

1. The term of the Agreement.
2. The circumstances in which it may be extended and by whom.
3. Ways in which it may be terminated prematurely and by whom.
4. Premises which the customer is to make available.
5. Premises which the contractor agrees to make available.

6. Any undertakings by either side to take over existing buildings including their leases.

7. Definitions of computer hardware and software systems which are the subject matter of the agreement: what is to happen to each?

8. Definitions of groups of staff affected by the agreement. Are any changes of employer envisaged, or undertakings regarding preservation of benefits, pensions and other matters in accordance with current employment law? The Transfer of Undertakings (Protection of Employment) Regulations, known colloquially as 'TUPE', apply here. With TUPE and with the sensitive human issues involved in any changes of employer, this is generally reckoned to be one of the more delicate areas of outsourcing. It calls for careful handling by experienced people.

9. Definitions of intellectual property. This includes patented hardware, copyright software both owned and under licence. What is to happen to each? Are there any specific arrangements for seeking novations to contracts with other parties?

10. Novations of contract in general. 'Novation' is the process of replacing one party to a contract with another. Normally it can only be achieved by agreement between all of the parties to the original contract. These may be necessary with suppliers and possibly with customers. Typically there will be an obligation upon the customer to procure such novations as may be necessary for the contractor to execute its tasks.

11. Performance criteria. These tend to be crucial in any outsourcing contract. What levels of system performance are deemed acceptable by the customer. Sometimes levels of payment to the contractor are linked to performances achieved.

12. Time breaks. Sometimes there will be provision for a contract or performance review after a specified period, so that each party may review its needs in the light of practical experience.

13. Codes of practice. There may be undertakings by the contractor to abide by specified industry codes of practice.

14. Variation order procedures. These can form a key element in agreements of this kind.

15. Confidentiality undertakings. These may apply in suitable terms to both sides. There may also be clauses obliging each side to declare and/or to avoid conflicts of interest while the agreement is in force. Each party may have to agree to honour non-disclosure obligations which the other party may have to third parties.

16. Liability and indemnity. Clauses covering this area need to be carefully drafted, bearing in mind the risk management profile of each party. Typically the contractor will seek to avoid liability for any indirect or consequential loss or damage, especially that arising from the business in which the customer is conducting. The customer on its part will be considering what protection it needs from the non-performance by its key contractor. Frequently there will be a liquidated damages clause against the contractor, since this can be evaluated in advance in terms of risk.

17. Early termination. Whilst there will be the usual premature termination clauses to cover insolvency, non-payment, or non-performance by either side, consideration needs to be given to the practicalities of terminating early. These can be quite intricate in operational terms.

18.   Dispute resolution. In view of the fiduciary relationship which inevitably develops between the parties to outsourcing contracts (and without which, arguably, they should not proceed) provision may be made for initial internal dispute resolution 'by representatives from each side not associated with the project'. Subsequent recourse may be had to ADR (alternative dispute resolution), arbitration or else to law.

19.   Consideration. The whole question of consideration is complex. Frequently a position is taken that the benefits from the agreement should be shared out between both parties, since part of the outsourcing philosophy is akin to that of a joint venture. Formulae which arrive at such mutual benefits need to be carefully thought out. If the contract is of many years' duration, index-linking of prices and costs may be necessary. The key here is to choose the right indices, possibly with review processes at stated intervals.

20.   Broader issues. In some of the larger outsourcing agreements, arrangements may be made for one side to assimilate one or more subsidiary companies of the other. In such cases specialist advice is needed so that appropriate 'due diligence' processes may be carried out in advance of any transfer.

Summary

Sales of goods and services

1.   Be aware of the law if you sell goods.
2.   Understand the terms 'satisfactory quality' and 'fitness for purpose'.
3.   Be especially aware if your organisation sells to the general public in their private capacity as 'consumers'.
4.   Remember the key factors: ownership of property, risk and its transfer, delivery, and payment. Know the remedies when things go wrong.
5.   Are the goods correctly described? Bear in mind the Trade Descriptions Act.
6.   Update yourself on the Unfair Contract Terms provisions of July 1995 where you supply goods direct to consumer. If you supply goods to consumers, consider a legal advice 'health check' upon your practices and documentation.

Outsourcing

1.   Outsourcing is a specialist area; if in doubt, take advice!
2.   It usually involves two organisations working closely together, or else the one taking over an integral part of the other's procedures. Be sure that is what your own organisation wants, and that both parties are, or could be, compatible.
3.   Consider whether you have in-house specialist services which might better be performed by an organisation whose 'core business' includes that specialisation. If so, outsourcing may be for you.
4.   Examine the benefits and the costs carefully.
5.   If all seems well, then proceed — with due caution and realism!

9

Agency

Most contractual matters in companies are dealt with by employees. An employee is an agent of the company when he acts in that capacity. Hence it is important that we are generally familiar with the law of agency.

What is an agent?

An agent is a person engaged to bring about contractual relationships between the person who appointed him and another party or parties. The appointor of the agent is known as the principal. It is a curious fact that since the agent does not enter into the contract, he does not need to have the capacity to do so. Hence a minor or an undischarged bankrupt may act as agent. The important part is that the principal should have the required capacity, whatever that might be. There are three basic ways in which an agency can be created:

1. By explicit agreement between the agent and the principal.
2. It can be implied by conduct.
3. It can be deemed to arise out of necessity.

Agencies by explicit agreement

An agreement between the principal and the agent need not be in writing. Clearly it is wiser that there should be a written agency agreement, but it is not essential. If, however, the agent is to be empowered to enter into a contract under seal on behalf of the principal, then he needs a power of attorney to enable him to do so. The power of attorney will have to be under seal, and in the case of a company granting the power this will have to be executed in accordance with the Articles, and witnessed normally by two directors, or one director and the company secretary.

If the power of attorney is to be executed abroad, it may be necessary to have it notarised. In some overseas jurisdictions this requires processes involving the Foreign and Commonwealth Office and the consulate of the foreign government concerned, as well as the procedures of the notary. This can take some days, and time needs to be allowed for it. Powers of attorney are subject to the Powers of Attorney Act.

Agencies implied by conduct

If someone maintains either by words or by conduct that another person has authority to commit him in contract, the person purporting to place the authority will be deemed to be the principal and the other person will be the agent. One example would be when the supposed principal regularly pays bills incurred by the other party.

The other instance, which is much closer to the subject of this book, is when an employee holds himself out to third parties to have authority by using titles such as 'contracts manager', 'sales manager', 'buyer'. In such cases, if the employer acquiesces by honouring purchase orders, sales orders, and other actions – even verbal commitments by such people – then an agency situation will usually be deemed to exist.

At one time a wife was supposed to have an implied agency to commit her husband's assets to buy necessary goods, which is how the term 'common law wife'[1] arose, since the agency had nothing to do with the existence or otherwise of marriage vows. The husband had various possible redresses, including the giving of specific notice to suppliers that his wife was no longer authorised as his agent. A trading company has this practical redress also. It is quite usual to find purchasing departments circulating all those suppliers listed in their bought ledgers, warning them that only those invoices backed by official purchase orders will be settled.

A partner in a business trading as a partnership has authority to act as agent for the partnership, unless notice is given to the contrary.

Agencies arising out of necessity

There may be instances when an agency is created -or more usually extended – due to special circumstances of necessity. This may arise where a party has first been entrusted with goods. Owing to a special situation, such as damage to a ship at sea needing urgent repair, or – in one legal case – there being no one available to receive livestock at the end of a journey, such an agency is created. The person entrusted with the goods is obliged to take reasonable steps to preserve them. To do this he may incur expenditure and may even pledge the goods to obtain credit, even though all of this was previously beyond his authority. There are, however, some constraints:

1.   There must not be another agent available who has the requisite authority.
2.   It must be impossible to contact the principal and get instructions from him.
3.   There must be a real need – usually some kind of emergency – such as might arise with vessels at sea, aircraft or goods which might perish. Local convenience is not enough.
4.   The agent of necessity must act in good faith, for the benefit of all those who may be concerned.

---

[1] It might be worth recording that, apart from the special and now out-dated legal meaning, the term 'common law wife' has no significance whatsoever in law! Some laws, however, do have application to those living as husband and wife.

It may be of interest to consider how this law may affect employees, who are obliged to act with due diligence in respect of their employer's affairs. One management college used to summarise it thus:

Question: An emergency arises at work, typically on a Friday night. Your common sense tells you that certain action is needed fast to rectify it, but you do not have the budgetary authority. Your boss has gone home, so have the directors, and no one else is around who has any more authority than you do. Yet the problem will not wait. What should you do?

Answer: Use your presence of mind, having discussed it, perhaps, with any colleagues at hand who have relevant knowledge or experience. Then take the necessary action, regardless of the budget. Afterwards, report the matter to the appropriate authority at the first opportunity, and seek further instructions.

The following is a real-life instance from the author's experience.

A company demerger took place involving transfer of staff and company cars. The documents were signed on the afternoon before a Bank Holiday weekend. The contracts manager for various reasons had not been involved in the processes. He was later informed that the deal had been struck, and it suddenly became apparent to him that a considerable part of the demerged sales force was about to drive away on holiday whilst technically uninsured, since the ownership of their vehicles had just transferred to a newly formed company without fleet cover. Both negotiating teams had gone home, and so had everybody else. There were ten minutes left in which to ring the underwriters and fix temporary cover on behalf of the other company. He did so!

Although the moral of the story is possibly to have mobile telephones issued to all, and to have everyone keep checklists of home telephone numbers and 'whom to ring' lists in their wallets, real life has a way of serving up emergency situations from time to time. Every serving soldier is taught how to assume command in a situation when his superiors are disabled in battle. The law and practice of 'agencies of necessity' could with profit be read and understood by us all.

Ratifying the acts of agents

Save in the special case of agencies of necessity, if an agent acts beyond his authority, the resultant contract will not be binding upon his principal. This often happens as a result of some technicality or error in the documentation.

In such a case, the principal will wish to confirm the act of the agent. This confirmation, known as ratification, is itself subject to a series of rules, many of which have arisen as a result of specific cases.

The rules for ratification may be summarised thus:

1.   Ratification may itself either be expressed, or it may be implied by the conduct of the principal.
2.   The principal must have had the capacity to have entered into the contract both at the time when the agent entered into it erroneously *and* at the time of ratification. In the case of a company, for instance, it must have had its Certificate of Incorporation no later than the earlier of the two dates. If the agent contracted on behalf of the company before it was formed, then he is in the special position of an agent who had no principal. He becomes personally liable as if he had contracted for himself.
3.   When ratifying, the principal must either be aware of all the significant facts about the contract, *or else* be prepared to honour the contract whatever those facts may be.
4.   The agent must have disclosed the fact of his agency to the other party. If he did not disclose the existence of a principal, and in fact had no authority to act as agent anyway, then ratification is not possible.
5.   Only the principal who was named, or whose identity could have been established at the time, may ratify.

If ratification is not possible under the above rules, it is of course always possible for the principal to start all over again and execute a contract with the other party. The point about ratification, however, is that when it is possible the contract automatically dates back to the original date when the agent brought it about. In a renegotiation, this backdating might not be possible and certainly will not be possible if the other party does not agree.

The authority of agents

The existence and extent of agents' authority has long been a matter for concern in commerce, and there have been numerous legal cases on the subject. The first point to be made is that there are two aspects to authority: the degree of authority that the agent actually has, and the degree of *ostensible* authority which he displays to third parties. The problems begin to arise when the two degrees of authority are different.

In a trading company the job title and general demeanour which the employee is permitted to display (such as the size of his office and the model of his company car) may influence the degree of authority which outside bodies may reasonably deem him to have. A managing director, for instance, will be deemed to have more authority than a manager, and much more authority – say – than a book-keeping assistant who might be presumed to have little or no authority at all. In each case the employing company is bound by the acts of its staff acting within their ostensible authority, unless notice has first been given to the counterparties restricting that authority, declaring what the level of authority actually is.

There have been some specific cases which only partially clarify the picture. In 1971 a case involving a company secretary established that he certainly had sufficient authority to arrange car hire. There was, however, a curious case in 1983 between the British Bank of the Middle East and the Sun Life Assurance Company of Canada (UK). In that case, the Bank sought assurances from the general manager of the Assurance Company that a particular branch official had authority for a specific transaction normally undertaken by a senior official. Two written replies were sent confirming his authority, *not* from the Head Office but from a branch manager. Relying upon this, a contract was executed which the Assurance Company later successfully repudiated. It was held that the written replies, not coming from someone in a position to give such assurances, were invalid even though they were on company notepaper and in reply to a letter to a senior officer. It should be mentioned that the transaction was of a non-routine kind.

Much day-to-day business is conducted in the absence of concern about authority, and most of it is quite sound. It might be helpful, however, to bear in mind the following 'five star guide'. The more stars, the higher the level of reassurance.

The five star guide on authority

★ Verbal undertaking of an employee with ostensible authority. Quite valid, provided we can prove it if we have to.

★★ Simple contract in writing. Perfectly adequate for most purposes.

★★★ Document under seal. This becomes serious stuff. It will bear the signature of two directors, or one director and a secretary, and it will bear the common seal which is the instrument of the board. Essential for many classes of transaction, notably conveyances of land, powers of attorney, and contracts with certain statutory bodies which can only contract under seal. In practice it would be very difficult indeed for a company to repudiate a deed.

★★★★ Document under seal, with a certified copy of the board resolution authorising or ratifying the use of the seal. This clearly commits the whole board of directors to the document, and puts the validity almost beyond question (note the special case of companies which do not use a seal, dealt with in Chapter 2).

★★★★★ All of the above 'four star' documentation plus the original copy of Companies House form 395 or 397 for presentation at Companies House. This is a 'special case' since it only applies to legal charges of a kind whose validity suffers if the form is presented late. Typically this device is used by banks to ensure that far-reaching controls over the assets of the company are adequately protected before financial support is given. It serves, however, to complete our 'five star guide'.

One effect of these cases has been an increase in the frequency with which the company secretary's office will be asked for formal assurances about executives levels of authority. It can be important that a central file of authority levels is kept readily available.

What is a special agent?

Use of the term 'special agent' in thriller fiction tends to deflect attention from the fact that it is a term with defined legal meaning. An agent authorised to complete one transaction or contract is known as a special agent. An agent authorised to carry on a particular section of the business is known as a general agent. General agents have implied authority to do whatever is involved in running their part of the business, whereas special agents have authority just for their specific assignments. Managing directors and general managers are general agents. The holder of a power of attorney will be a special agent, at least in respect of that power.

There are certain variations of detail in the law and practice as it applies to specific kinds of agency. Notable among these are estate agencies and auctioneers, debt factors, and various classes of broker. Some agents are appointed on the basis that they are responsible for the financial probity of the counterparties they introduce. Such agents are known as '*del credere* agents'.

What are an agent's duties?

An agent has the following duties in law:

1. To act with due diligence in carrying out his agency.
2. To use any skill which he claims to have.
3. If he is a selling agent, he must conclude at the best price he can get, even if this means withdrawing from 'subject to contract' engagements which are not yet binding.
4. He must disclose to the principal any material facts he becomes aware of which might influence the proposed deal.
5. He must not have a conflict of interest. Hence he may not himself become the counterparty.
6. He must provide an account when asked.
7. He must not profit beyond the agreed figure or scale of figures. If he does, the amount is disclosable and is the property of the principal.

If the agent should take any secret profits or 'backhanders', then the principal may:

1. Recover the secret profit, *and*
2. Refuse to pay the agency fee or commission, *and*
3. Summarily dismiss the agent, *and*
4. Repudiate the contract.

The principal has specific rights of action both against the agent and the party offering the bribe, both of whom are criminally liable. The agent, however, is not under a duty to disclose his breaches to the principal as such, and the burden of proof lies with the principal.

An agency is a personal relationship, so that the agent may not employ anyone else to carry out his agency without the principal's consent.

What are a principal's duties?

The principal has duties:

1.   To pay the agent.
2.   To indemnify the agent for acts lawfully carried out within (but not beyond) the scope of his authority as an agent.

How can an agency be ended?

An agency can be terminated by the act of the parties. Typically this will be by mutual agreement, though the principal may elect to revoke the agent's powers. If this involves a breach of contract, the usual remedies will apply in damages. Revocation, however, is limited. It will only be effective against third parties if and when those parties have been informed of it. It will not be effective at all if the agency income forms part of consideration due under an ancillary contract. Hence if book debts are sold with an authority to act as agent in collecting them as part of the price, then that agency is irrevocable.

Agencies can also be terminated by law in the following ways:

1.   Death of the principal.
2.   Bankruptcy of the principal.
3.   Mental incapacity of the principal (save in the special case of an enduring power of attorney).
4.   The principal becomes an enemy (and thereby automatically making most of the agent's acts illegal and possibly treasonable).

Mental incapacity terminates the agency but does not affect commitments to third parties until they have been informed of the incapacity.

The commercial agent

Having said all this, it must be stated that the law has been greatly changed as regards *commercial* agents by the Commercial Agents (Council Directive) Regulations 1993 (S.I. 1993/No. 3053), which came into force on 1 January 1994.

Here the term 'commercial agent' means a self-employed intermediary who has continuing authority to negotiate the sale or purchase of goods on behalf of his or her principal, or to negotiate and conclude the sale. It expressly excludes officers of a company or partners in a partnership exercising their authority, and insolvency practitioners, together with one or two other categories including agents who do not get paid for their activities.

The regulations expressly lay down the following rights and obligations:

Duties of a commercial agent to his principal

1.   He must look after the principal's interests and act dutifully and in good faith.
2.   He must make proper efforts to negotiate and – where appropriate – to conclude the transactions he is instructed to take care of. He must communicate all necessary available information to his principal, and must comply with all reasonable instructions which the principal gives him.

Duties of a principal to his commercial agent

1.   He must likewise act dutifully and in good faith toward the agent.
2.   In particular he must provide the agent with the necessary documentation relating to the goods, he must obtain for the agent any information necessary for him to perform, and must notify the agent within a reasonable time if he expects that the volume of transactions will be significantly below expectations.
3.   He must also inform the agent within a reasonable time of his acceptance, refusal, or failure to execute a commercial transaction which the agent has introduced.

Neither side may derogate from these obligations, and if they do so the law applicable to the contract shall apply to any breaches.

   In addition, the regulations cover in considerable detail the following subjects:

(a) The form and amount of remuneration, in the absence of agreement.
(b) Entitlement to commission on transactions concluded during the agency contract.
(c) Entitlement to commission after the agency contract has ended.
(d) Apportionment of commission between new and previous commercial agents.
(e) When commission becomes due and when payable.
(f) Extinction of right to commission.
(g) Periodic supply of information on commission due, and agent's right to inspect principal's books.
(h) Both parties' right to a signed written statement of terms.
(i) What happens when an agency agreement continues to be performed after expiry.
(j) Minimum periods of notice.
(k) Agent's entitlement to indemnity or compensation upon termination (and grounds for exclusion or such entitlement).
(l) Restraint of trade clauses.

Any agreement to derogate from specified parts of these items, to the detriment of the agent, will be void.

   The above is merely a summary of the content of the Regulations, which can be obtained at modest cost from HMSO and are fortunately written in fairly simple English. The advent of these regulations, which have in many ways revolutionised the position of the commercial agents, means that professional legal advice really should be obtained by anyone who has not extensive and recent knowledge in that area. This is especially so in the early years before experience has been gained in interpretation.

Some special situations arising from agents' contracts

When the agent enters into a contract acting on behalf of a known principal, then he is not liable on the contract, unless it is the custom of the trade that he should be liable. The rights and obligations flow directly between the two principals. If, however, the agent signs a deed in his own name, he is liable on it, which is an example of the added solemnity of deeds, and its legal effect. Even if the agent does not disclose the name of the principal, as long as he is overtly contracting as an agent, he avoids liability.

An agent contracting ostensibly as a principal on the face of the contract will normally incur personal liability, even if it subsequently transpires that the counterparty knew at the time that he was an agent. In such cases the other party may sue either party in the event of a cause of action arising. This is why it is often desirable in formal offer and acceptance correspondence for staff to sign 'for and on behalf of XYZ Limited'.

Where the agent does not disclose that he is dealing as an agent at all – a 'secret agent' in effect – he naturally becomes liable to the other party as a principal. However, the real principal retains the right to reveal himself in such cases and, where applicable, to sue the other party in his own right. In that event the real principal becomes personally liable. The third party in such cases may choose which of the other two to hold to account, although once he has made a choice he cannot alter it.

Conclusion   The law of agency is closely related in practice to contractual matters. This is especially true since employed staff are agents. Although much of employment law today is governed by statute, the principles of agency apply to much of what staff are able to do in binding the company to outside bodies. The underlying principles should be clearly understood by all contracts staff.

Summary

1. An agent is someone authorised to arrange a contract, or to carry on a business, for someone else. Most employees are in some respects agents for their firms or companies.
2. Agencies may be expressed by written contract, or they may be implied by contract, or they may arise in emergencies.
3. It can be important that an agent's actual authority is the same as his ostensible authority. Usually a principal will be bound by the agent's ostensible authority.
4. Note the special situation of the commercial agent, and have a copy of the

commercial agents (Council Directive) Regulations 1993 (S.I. 1993/No. 3053) — and a good lawyer — available.

5. If an agent acts beyond his authority, there are rules which govern whether or not the principal may later back him up and ratify. If he can ratify, then the ratification is dated back to the time of the unauthorised act. If not, then the principal may have to start all over again with the other party.

6. An agent must act in good faith. If he does not, then the principal may summarily dismiss him.

10
Intellectual property

What is intellectual property?

Intellectual property is an intangible asset of a business, yet it can be of vital importance. It can affect rights and freedoms of enterprises to manufacture and sell, both at home and abroad. It can affect marketing strategies and it can restrict the uses to which certain information is put.

A major problem in many companies is identifying it and managing it, and for that reason it is of concern to the contracts manager. Without understanding the subject it is not difficult to promise to others that which we do not have the right to promise, and to fail to obtain from others rights which can be essential to us. Part of the problem is that those who create it tend to be creative, and they do not know a great deal about the law.

The term originally used was 'industrial property', signifying the branch of law which was devoted to intangibles in the manufacturing sector and related fields. With the growth of valuable know-how in other areas, notably performing rights in the entertainment industry and computer software, the whole subject has been widened. It is perhaps important to realise that the term intellectual property or intellectual property rights (IPR) has no general agreed legal definition. Thus it can mean whatever we decide that it shall mean in a given context.

There are, of course, two separate aspects to the subject: the property itself, and the rights to it which may include exploitation. Let us now consider the various kinds of property which commonly fall within the generally agreed definition of the subject.

A first and fairly basic distinction should be made between those intellectual property categories which are or can be registered and those which cannot.

Registered property

Registered IPR is in most countries regulated by statute law. Public registers are kept to indicate what rights have been established, or are being applied for. They will also indicate who owns the property or who is claiming to own it.

● **Patent rights:** Patent rights are perhaps the best known of intellectual property rights in that elaborate provisions are made for their establishment and protection. Many household articles bear patent registration numbers or the legend 'Pat. Applied For'. Patents, however, are not suitable for all classes of innovation, as we shall discuss.

- **Trade marks:** Trade marks, which cover goods and services, afford protection for company names, brand names and marks of distinction, provided they are used in trading. Registration is possible in most countries of the world, subject to various detailed provisions.
- **Registered designs:** A registered design is a registerable intellectual property which offers protection of an article's appearance, which must 'appeal to the eye', as against its underlying invention.

Patents

A patent is in essence a protection under statute law. It offers protection for an invention, and the period is normally 20 years. A key feature of patent protection is that, in return for the benefits which registration confers, the invention must be *disclosed*. Early in the registration process a significant amount of information becomes public knowledge, so that secrecy is lost.

There is no such thing as an international patent. Patents are *territorial*, so that one has to decide whether to protect overseas as well as in the home country. Typically we might decide to protect in all those countries which have a sufficiently advanced industry to be able to replicate and to market infringing articles.

In the UK, as in most other countries, there has to be the concept of *Industrial Application* for a patent to succeed. Patents are not granted for items of literature or the arts. Even computer software has normally been patented as part of industrial hardware, though here the law has become complex and subject to change. Under the Patents Act of 1977 it was established that an invention was capable of industrial application if it can be made or used in any kind of industry, including agriculture.

There must be *novelty*. The technical concept must be new as at the initial date of filing or submission to the Patent Office. This is important. If the invention has been published before that date it may be claimed that it is no longer new, and the patent application can fail. A disclosure in confidence, however, is not fatal and there are some special rules which apply to unauthorised disclosures. There are slight differences in this area between the UK and other countries, notably the USA.

There has to be an *inventive step*. This is not always easy to define. It may hinge upon technical evidence. Mere novelty on its own is not enough. The invention must not be obvious. It must be something beyond that which a skilled workman, craftsman, or other member of staff might have been expected to try out in the normal course of developing his technological approach. Yet 'perspiration' in reaching the inventive step can be as significant as the sudden flash of creative 'inspiration', so that meticulous experimentation to reach the goal may be rewarded. The key point is that the result could not have been easily arrived at by someone skilled in the craft or technology.

Various classes of item are *excluded* from patentability. These encompass discoveries, scientific theories and mathematical methods. In the UK and most of the countries of Europe one cannot patent artistic works, methods for performing mental tasks, business methods or games, or ways of presenting information.

Patented inventions may not be *immoral, anti-social* or *offensive*. In most countries it is possible to patent chemical compounds, but not in Latin America. Likewise, in most countries, and notably in the UK and Europe it is not possible to patent methods of diagnosis or therapy, nor methods of treating human beings or animals. These are not restricted from patent protection in USA.

Methods of feeding human beings or animals *are* patentable, although the law is changing here. One can patent *cosmetic treatment*, but not if it is therapeutic.

In most countries biological methods such as genetically engineering a modified species may *not* be patented, but in USA this may be allowed. Special provisions exist for micro-organisms, plant protection and for biological inventions.

There must be *adequate disclosure*. This must be at the outset. Usually it is adequate if a specification is disclosed including sufficient data for someone normally skilled in the appropriate expert field to reproduce the process. There must be disclosure sufficiently broad to support the broadest scope for protection that one is seeking however.

In the USA the rules for disclosure are higher than those in the UK. In the USA it is wise to ensure that both the actual invention is detailed, and also the problems solved by it. In many countries one is obliged to disclose the best method of carrying out or using the invention.

Opposition to a grant of patent may be made by a third party intervening to prevent the grant. This normally happens within a period of three months after the Grant of Patent. An organisation with concerns in this matter needs an adequate watching service and an adequate internal decision making process to ensure that action is taken within the period.

The normal *duration* of a patent is 20 years from the date of application. Since in the UK one can re-file within one year of first filing, this gives effective protection for 21 years. In USA the term is 17 years after the Grant, which is normally made three years after application. In India, however, the period of protection is only seven years. UK patents include protection in Northern Ireland and the Isle of Man, but not in the Channel Islands, where separate filing is necessary. In most countries third parties are not permitted to use the invention between the time of application and the time of the grant. Although the proprietor cannot sue for infringement until after the grant, one can normally obtain damages afterwards. In practice it is usually possible to license use of the invention during the waiting period.

It can be important to *identify the individual inventors* even if they are staff members operating under a contract of service whereby their inventions belong to the enterprise. It can also be important to *keep in touch* with them. In some countries, such as the USA, the original recorded inventors may be called upon to sign patent documents even though they have clearly signed over the rights to the company and even though they may have left the company by that time.

It is as well to have clauses in their employment contracts which require cooperation at company expense, and that those clauses are drafted so as to survive termination.

In government and other contracting situations the terms *background* and *foreground* are sometimes used in connection with intellectual property. *Background* is the term used to refer to intellectual property which is either pre-existing or is being developed independent of the contract itself. *Foreground* is intellectual property which is being developed specifically for the contract in hand. According to the method of funding the ownership of background may well be different from the ownership of foreground. Whatever the contract may state, certain classes of intellectual property can be declared as available for *Crown use*, typically for defence of the realm.

Steps to securing a patent

The following steps are taken to secure a patent:

1. *Prepare an abstract*. This is rather like the preamble to a contract. It is not part of the patent when granted, but it summarises the nature of the invention. It is there to help members of the public in their searches.
2. *Prepare description*. The disclosure rules have to be borne in mind. In addition there must be a statement of the relationship that the invention bears to prior knowledge in that area of technique, especially for US patents. Once submitted it is not normally possible to add anything to the description. There is a period of one year during which this document is tabled for examination, during which one can re-file. After that, the patent is granted.
3. *Claims*. The question of claims is technical, and a matter for patent specialists. Claims are definitions of the technology. They define the broadest concept of the invention, and its applications. Drafting of this documentation can be crucial in enabling effective enforcement and exploitation at a later stage.

The steps to a grant of patent are:

(a) Prepare the application.
(b) Formal submission to the Patent Office.
(c) The official search. The patent examiner will examine the application and carry out a search.
(d) Publication.
(e) Payment of the examination fee.
(f) Examination report.
(g) Correspondence.
(h) The grant itself.

A typical elapsed time period for all of this might be 2–3 years. After the first year, the foreign filings would commence.

What is the cost of a patent?

As a very rough guide the cost of a patent may be taken as between £300 and £500 per country per year, to which should be added agents' fees, watching services, and the costs of being challenged and of challenging others. There are also possible legal proceedings. One recent patent application involving several overseas countries cost £10,000 in fees and expenses, plus quite a lot of internal, technical and managerial time. Costs tend to ease off as the life of the grant proceeds.

Trade marks

Trade marks are registerable. A trade mark is a symbol which the public can recognise and associate with certain goods or services, so as to incline them to have confidence in the product and wish to purchase it. It can be a word, or a symbol or device, or even an identifiable aspect of the goods themselves. In most countries trade mark rights depend upon registration. Unregistered trade marks are protected only by the tort of 'passing off'. Registered protection is better.

There are various classes of registration. Failure to register in a given class of use will deny protection in that class. However, since November 1994 the Trade Marks Act 1994 has allowed those with a UK reputation to sue others who use their mark in non-registered classes where unfair advantage is taken of the registered mark, or where use is detrimental to the registered mark.

The EU member countries and the USA also permit registration of marks for services. Whereas a trade mark passes with the goods from hand to hand, a service mark relates to transactions between two parties, such as banking, insurance or consultancy. The 1994 Act abolished the term 'service mark' and the EU Trade Marks Directive requires all EU states to provide registration for marks for goods and services.

The *duration* of a mark is indefinite, for as long as it is kept in force and provided the renewal fees are paid every 10 years.

To be *acceptable*, a mark must be distinguishable from those of other traders.

Manner of use

The ways in which trade and service marks are used can be of importance. It is sometimes said that the mark *should always be used as an adjective and not as a noun*. Hence on all printed brochures one would refer to an 'ABC Vacuum Cleaner' and never shorten it to an 'ABC'. Once a certain type of vacuum cleaner became widely known merely as an 'ABC' it could be held that the name was generic and therefore not protectable.

It is wise to ensure that there is always a footnote in printed material referring to the fact the 'ABC is a registered trade mark owned by ABC Manufacturing Limited'. Sometimes the devices ™ or ® may be used. In the UK ® means Registered Trade Mark, and ™ means that an application has been made, *or* that the mark is unregistered but could be protected by the common law right of passing off as to trading name.

Choosing a trade mark

Here are some key actions to take in choosing a trade mark:

(a) Choose a good trade mark agent.
(b) Brief him or her on your business.
(c) Establish an internal procedure whereby anyone introducing and naming a new product or service first furnishes details. You will need to know:
  (i) Brief details of product or service.
  (ii) Market areas expected over the next five years or so (countries, not districts).
  (iii) Volume of expected business over that period, in terms of quantity and value.
  (iv) Up to six proposed names in order of preference (more choices than this if common or 'obvious' names are being sought as there is a greater risk of their not being available).
  (v) Whose budget is going to pay for it (optional!).

Trade and service marks are less expensive than patents to register. A 'round figure' estimate might be £500 per class per country, plus agents' fees. It is wise, however, to obtain estimates in advance. Renewal fees of a lower cost arise every 10 years in the EU according to the country, and there are always 'unknowns' in the form of legal fees for challenges issued and received.

Registered designs

In contrast with patents, where the protection is for inventors, the registered design focuses upon appearance. It is that which it seeks to protect. If anyone is seeking to use a similar design it is sufficient merely to compare the appearance of the two to establish whether an infringement might be about to occur.

The owner of a registered design may be:

(a) The author.
(b) The party who commissioned it.
(c) The employer, if it was designed by a staff member.
(d) An assignee of someone who has a good title.

The other facets of a registered design are:

- It must be *novel*. It must not have previously been registered or published within the UK.
- It must be *applied by an industrial process* of some kind.
- It must *appeal to the eye*.
- The design must comprise *pattern*, *shape*, *ornament* or *configuration*.

If the applicable article is a part of something else, then one cannot register the part only. The whole must be registerable. The design might previously have been copyright, but that is no bar to registration unless the previous copyright work had been applied industrially.

The shape of a registered design must not have been solely dictated by its function, so that it had to be that shape anyway. There must be *something beyond the functional minimum* even if that extra attribute has itself some functional use. It must be aesthetically appealing and will not be protected where that part for which registration is sought must fit or match with another item; hence car body parts and exhaust pipes are not protected.

Consequences of registration

Registration gives the owner exclusive right in the UK against anyone else to make, import, sell, offer for sale, or hire the article. If the work is reproduced industrially – which is one of the preconditions – then protection lasts for 25 years from the end of the calendar year of first marketing.

Unregistered property

There is, however, a significant body of property which, though unregisterable, is nonetheless real and protectable IPR in law, though its intangibility can make control difficult.

- **Copyright:** With the significant growth of the entertainment industry in this century, notably publishing in all its forms, the theatre, radio, television, and computer software, copyright assertion and protection has become very big business in its own right. So much so that there are performing and other rights protection societies, a Federation Against Software Theft, and other faculties to ensure that royalties are properly obtained and the law enforced. The uses of the office photocopier and the uses to which blank audio or video cassettes are put, even in the home, are subject to copyright law.
- **Design rights:** Design rights, as distinct from registered designs, are rights under UK law. They protect functional, three-dimensional designs. They were created under the 1988 Copyright, Designs and Patents Act as a new concept.
- **Trade secrets and confidential information:** Trade secrets may include secret product formulations, customer sales or mailing lists. This aspect of IPR law may affect staff both during their contract of service and after they leave.
- **Unfair competition:** The rights and protections stemming from anti-trust or anti-monopoly legislation can have implications in the field of intellectual property.
- **Goodwill and reputation:** Goodwill comprises reputation, distinctive house style, and the manner in which marketing may be undertaken. An undertaking has the right of protection against a competitor seeking to pass himself off as part of the organisation, by imitation of a kind likely to mislead the public.

Copyright

One of the most commonly invoked classes of intellectual property is copyright. Copyright is not registerable, but is protected by statute law. It subsists in the concept of the 'concrete expression' of the author being preserved from the copying by others.

It is basically about the *right to copy*, and nothing else. To breach copyright one normally has copied the work without permission, whereas patents are infringed whether or not the infringer 'copied'. Computer software is covered by copyright.

Copyright does not pass with the ownership of the copy which has been made. It stays with the owner until – if ever – it has been assigned *in writing*.

The owner of a copyright is the author, unless that right is assigned to someone else who may have commissioned the work, except that work of employees produced in the course of employment are automatically owned by the employer without the need of an assignment. Under current law the author of a work has the right to be identified as such, but only if that right is asserted. This is known as one of the 'moral rights'. Moral rights do not, however, apply to computer programs.

There are three classes of copyright, each with different rules for the period of protection:

(a) *Original literature and works of music and art.* Protected for 50 years from the end of the calendar year in which the author dies. Extended to 70 years under an EU directive as from 1995, in respect of any copyright not expired anywhere in the EU at the time the directive became effective.
(b) *Sound recordings, films, broadcasts, and computer-generated works.* Protection here is for 50 years from the end of the year of first publication.
(c) *Typographical arrangements of works which have already been published.* Protection is for 25 years after the year of first publication.

Unregistered design right

Under the 1988 Copyright, Designs and Patents Act, an unregistered design right was introduced. This in effect modified earlier unregistered situations. The life of this unregistered right is 15 years. It protects a design of any aspect of a shape or configuration (internal or external) of the whole or part of an article. The designer must be a citizen of the UK or of one of the states of the European Union. The owner has exclusive right to copy or to make, but for the last five years of the protection period third parties have the right to acquire a licence. It only protects three-dimensional articles – not surface decoration, which may get registered design protection.

Trade secrets and confidential information

Trade secrets and other types of confidential information are in England a matter of common law. The following two points may be made in defining the situation:

(a) To be protectable, a secret must have *sufficient concrete reality* to give it a commercial value.
(b) To protect a secret there must be *a course of conduct which indicates a confidential relationship*. Within the UK this will more often than not arise

from the law of contract whereby one party receives confidential data from another in the course of a contractual relationship, and agrees to keep it secret.

One of the commonest areas whereby trade secrets are protected arises in a contract of employment. An employee owes his employer a duty of confidentiality which will survive the contract and the period of employment.

There is, however, powerful case law *preventing restraint of trade* which can inhibit some of the potential protection. For instance an employee cannot be prevented from taking with him his inherent skills some of which he will have acquired during his employment. This would not extend to a sales prospect list, in the event that the employee were a salesman.

Restraint of competition through the protection of confidential data from being used by ex-employees will sometimes be restricted by the courts to time periods or limits of geography which the particular court considers reasonable. Courts are always concerned to permit individuals to earn their living no matter how much know-how they might possess which may have been obtained in the service of others. A key question which will be put is 'What is the least restriction upon the individual which is reasonably necessary to protect the employer's legitimate interest?' Any restrictive clause in a contract which is significantly in excess of this may be curtailed or overridden.

There are three tests which should be put to establish whether there has been a breach of confidence:

1. Was the information actually confidential, and not in the public domain?
2. Was there a confidential relationship between the owner of the information and the alleged party in breach?
3. Was the information used in a way which was detrimental to the owner?

To avoid conflict with the first of these three principles, non-disclosure clauses in contracts are often drafted thus:

'A undertakes to hold in confidence the information made available to him hereunder save and to the extent that it is or shall become lawfully a matter of public knowledge'.

The term 'lawfully' excludes the unconscionable situation whereby something becomes public knowledge solely because of the breach of the clause itself by the defendant.

Exploiting intellectual property

In any discussion of intellectual property rights and their exploitation it should be mentioned that the whole subject of intellectual property is a deeply technical one. It demands careful study. In particular, the field of patents, design rights and trade marks normally require the services of skilled practitioners in those fields. Not only is one concerned with more than one legal code and overseas statutes, but – especially in the field of patents – an ancillary discipline is that of engineering. Specialist solicitors and Chartered Patent Agents are versed in this whole area and should be consulted.

Having made this caveat, there is no reason why the contracts practitioner should not make himself familiar in general terms with the subject, and in particular with ways of exploiting IPR.

Although it can be dangerous to take analogies too far, there are certain parallels between intellectual property and real property when it comes to matters of exploitation. The owner of a right can be likened to the freeholder of a large building, or possibly a leaseholder with so many years to run, depending upon the nature of the IPR. The property owner may sell his right to the building to someone, or he may grant tenancies for all or parts of the building in return for rent. Whilst the owner of IPR does not grant tenancies as such, he often does grant licences.

Licensing

To begin with, the owner may consider that 'the world is his oyster' as it were. He may licence someone to manufacture his patent, or to use his trade mark, or to reproduce his copyright material anywhere in the world. Subject to certain anti-trust provisions in the USA and the EU, he may appoint one licensee exclusively to exploit the right and pay royalties or commissions. That is known as an *exclusive licence*. Alternatively, he can grant a *non-exclusive licence*, allowing the same right to be held simultaneously – and possibly in competition – among several licensees. This can be likened to more than one tenant having access to common parts of a building, such as the lifts and the corridors.

The *entire right worldwide* may be licensed. Alternatively a licence may be granted for one or more continents or *territories*. Within each of those territories the grant might be exclusive or non-exclusive.

Grants need not be restricted by territory. They might be defined according to *markets*. One licensee might be granted the right to sell proprietary computer software to manufacturing companies, whereas another may be permitted to sell to the oil industry. This is sometimes known as '*horizontal*' as against '*vertical*' marketing.

The landlord of a building might grant his main tenants the right to sub-let all or part of the floors they occupy. In like manner the IPR proprietor might elect to grant his principal licensees the *right to sub-licence* and even to grant those sub-licensees rights to issue *secondary* or '*sub-sub*' licences. At each step these rights may be made exclusive or non-exclusive according to the circumstances.

Problems in licensing

So far everything remains relatively simple in analogy terms, save that it is much more difficult to keep track of what is happening in a market than in a building. Let us now consider a problem. Our oil industry licensee approaches one of the oil majors with worldwide networks of subsidiaries. The oil major is very interested in acquiring a licence on highly favourable terms to us. However, he insists upon a corporation-wide licence, embracing all of his subsidiaries throughout the world including numerous local joint ventures with other organisations. This is not unusual, yet it cuts across all our existing territorial structure.

If we have not contemplated this at the outset, we have an immediate problem which is not unlike that of the freeholder who grants more than one tenancy for the same part of the building. If we do not actually land ourselves in court, we shall certainly end up compensating some of our other licensees for loss of revenues within their territories.

Hence it can be important to commence with a global plan, whilst 'the world' is still ours to grant. This is primarily a marketing matter, but because it is often perceived as merely a legal or contractual technicality, we need to be on our guard and ready to warn appropriate colleagues when there is still time.

Undertakings

There is one more aspect to IPR exploitation which is not unlike that of real property – the passing across of covenants or undertakings which are necessary to allow the licensees to exploit without either grantor or grantee trespassing, as it were, upon other people's entitlements.

It is normal for the owner of the right to *warrant* to his licensees that he possesses that right. He will undertake to protect it from challenges by any third parties, if need be by legal action. He will *indemnify the licensees* from costs arising from actions by third parties claiming that they, and not he, owns the right. This he must do to enable any well-advised licensee to take up a licence. Indemnities are seldom unlimited, and it is sometimes possible to obtain title insurance to control a part of the risk. The usual provision however, is that whoever grants the indemnity insists upon *controlling the defence including any related settlements*, so that he who is obliged to 'pay the piper' does indeed 'call the tune' in terms of legal proceedings and their outcome.

To guard against insolvency and its effects upon licensees, the owner might feel obliged to enter into an '*escrow*' agreement. Typically this is an arrangement with a bank or professional association, with which a copy of any essential secret process is deposited. In the event of the licensor becoming insolvent or in some other prescribed ways being incapacitated, the escrow agent agrees upon request from the licensees to release such data as is essential for them to continue.

Most of the undertakings, however, will flow the other way. Each licensee will be obliged *to use the right in the terms laid down* by the owner, *to account for the use*, and *to declare and pay royalties* or other fees in accordance with that use. Often there is a right for *the owner to audit the books* of the licensee, or to procure a certificate from a practising public accountant. Frequently there will be a *right of entry* to the licensee's premises to ensure compliance, much like that which is found in landlord and tenant practice.

There will often be a requirement that any *trade mark or copyright notice* is correctly applied. Some or all of the material may be *supplied in confidence*, which might be made binding upon both licensees and their employees having access. There might also be a 'policing' clause whereby the licensee is obliged to *inform the owner of any perceived infringements* of which he may become aware. He might be obliged to assist the proprietor in the prosecution, or even to conduct that prosecution himself, especially if he and the infringer are in the same overseas territory.

He may be permitted *to make improvements or enhancements* to the product which is the subject of the grant, with or without undertaking to offer them to the owner either outright or by way of *reverse licence*. Some jurisdictions control matters such as this by statute.

If there is a right to sub-license, the owner will normally require that all *sub-licences are granted in terms acceptable* to him, and may require copies to be countersigned. All of these key regulatory clauses will need to be passed right down the line, so that the overall IPR is exploited in an orderly manner and royalties duly accounted for and passed back up the chain.

Although in strict legal terms an IPR licence is the grant of a right and not a contract as such, licences are almost always drawn up in the form of a licence agreement, so that both parties are bound in contract.

Key points to remember in licensing:

1. Never licence more than you own.
2. Keep the term of the licence shorter than the outstanding term of your IPR.
3. Draw a chart of your territories and keep it marked up with the grants you have made. Include a register of any sub-licences or secondary sub-licences and require that you are kept informed of all of these.
4. Decide early how you are going to exploit, and how you will handle 'special deals' when they arise.
5. Check that any licences comply with EU technology transfer regulations under EU competition law, which specifies in detail which are permitted and which are not under Article 85 of the Treaty of Rome.
6. Take care never to grant the same right more than once if it is 'exclusive'.
7. If you are licensee or sub-licensee, apply each of these rules in reverse. Is your title 'clean', and is the grantor taking care of the right he is granting you. Nobody gains from legal disputes.

Managing intellectual property rights

Managing IPR tends to vary a good deal from company to company. In some organisations, typically those with a high investment in research and development, managing intellectual property is very much part of the culture. There may be a manual of procedures. In each research laboratory there might be a researcher's notebook into which details of every new invention have to be copied. At regular intervals a patent officer might attend and examine the book. A Patent Committee then decides whether to register, and the procedures are put in place.

Such organisations may apply for patents or other protection for the following reasons:

1. To protect and exploit themselves.
2. To prevent others from exploiting.
3. With a view to licensing others to exploit, thus enhancing their own assets.

They may also conduct regular searches to determine:

4. That which they cannot exploit because it is being protected and possibly exploited by others.
5. That which they might exploit by negotiating a licence from others.
6. 'Bright ideas' for which, with care, they might develop non-infringing alternatives.

In other, faster moving organisations – notably the computer industry – such processes might not be so appropriate. Product life spans can be very short. Software is often obsolete within five years; hardware in an even shorter period.

To manage and protect IPR is costly. Trade mark and patent agents may be needed. The time of specialists has to be allowed for and costed. There are registration fees to pay, watching services to employ, and the whole affair takes up management time.

Sometimes it can be feasible to protect components rather than the complete product, since their intellectual value lasts longer. However, mixed discipline teams may be continually forming and disbanding when their tasks are done. To submit them to a rigorous and permanent discipline might be impractical. Manuals of procedure may be out of date before they can be issued.

In such cases one has to ask oneself some more basic questions about intellectual property and its significance; value analysis in fact. For example:

(a) Do we have know-how or original protectable work of significant value? Product names? Trade or service names? Copyright material?
(b) How much are they worth to us?
(c) How much are they worth to our competitors?
(d) What would it cost us if we lost the protection?
(e) How much could we gain by packaging and selling our IPR? Or licensing? Or using ourselves?
(f) How much would it cost to protect in order to do so? How much in terms of internal resources?
(g) How does all this fit into our overall business objectives?
(h) Bearing that in mind, what should we do?

Policing the rights

Having protected IPR, what are the best ways of policing the rights? On the basis that 'prevention is better than cure' a first rule might be to choose licensees or distributors with care. As far as possible one needs to avoid organisations without a clean business reputation to protect. Large corporations are sometimes to be preferred because their profile is too great for them to ignore the risks to themselves of being caught in the act of infringement. Smaller entities may have greater incentive to perform but greater caution needs to be taken in selecting them.

The main legal actions for infringement include actions to obtain damages and injunctions. An injunction can require the alleged infringer to *cease and desist* forthwith, pending a full court case. A particular form of injunction associated with intellectual property rights actions is known as the *Anton Piller Order*, named after the party involved in the first case in which it was used. This can be a powerful weapon against the infringer. Where the plaintiff has a *prima facie* indication that

1.   an infringement is occurring or is likely to occur, and
2.   the suspected infringer is of a character likely to dispose of evidence before a normal court hearing could occur,

then the plaintiff can seek an *ex parte* injunction, which means that representation is made to a High Court judge in chambers without the involvement or knowledge of the other side. If the judge sees fit, he may entitle the plaintiff by order of the court

3.   to visit all the places of business of the alleged infringer, including any other places where evidence might be held, including private homes, without prior notice,
4.   to serve upon the occupants of those premises a notice requiring them to allow immediate admittance to search and to seize any documents relevant to a full hearing, or
5.   to permit the recipients to delay entry only long enough to seek their own legal advice on the meaning of the injunction, during which time no property may be removed.

Because of the severity of an Anton Piller Order, which in some circumstances could ruin the defendant's business in advance of a court action (which the defendant might ultimately win), and because of the other aspects of the Order, there are usually certain protections awarded:

6.   The applicants may be required to provide significant guarantees or other sureties to the court so that in the event that their action fails, the defendants can obtain the substantial damages that they may well have suffered. Sometimes the defendants' solicitor will delay entry while this point is being established.
7.   The applicants must serve the Order with their own solicitors present, who are officers of the court.
8.   If the recipients are female, then it may be stipulated that a female solicitor must be present.
9.   Consideration has been given to a requirement that at least one solicitor be involved who is familiar with these injunctions; practice is developing in this area.

Injunctions of this kind raise serious issues for both sides. They are never to be engaged upon lightly, since they can bring financial collapse to the party that loses, but the fact that such legal instruments exist should be sufficient reminder that IPR infringement can be serious. Breach of an injunction, as we have said elsewhere, is contempt of court which can sometimes result in gaol sentences even though the original breach was a civil matter.

Recent developments in intellectual property law

Following the introduction of European Council Directive No. 93/98/EEJ in July 1995, a draft Statutory Instrument was laid before Parliament on 20 November 1995. After clearance by both Houses, it took effect from 1 January 1996. It deals with:

1. Copyright
2. Rights in performances
3. Publication right

In summary, it lays down circumstances in which a principal director of a film can also be treated as author of the film. Where that director is an employee, then the employer can be the first owner of the copyright.

The duration of copyright for literary, dramatic, musical and artistic works is extended to 70 years. Copyright in a film expires at the end of the period of 70 years or from the end of the calendar year in which the death occurs of the last to die of the persons connected with the film. There is a change to the definition of 'released' in relation to sound recordings.

There are reciprocal provisions for the duration of copyright where the author or the country of origin of a literary, dramatic, musical or artistic work is outside the European Union. A section deals with anonymous and pseudonymous works, and extension to the jurisdiction of the Copyright Tribunal.

Provisions are introduced regarding publication rights as they affect original literary, dramatic, musical and artistic works, and films. There are transitional provisions relating to works created before the implementation date of the Statutory Instrument. There is also a lengthy explanatory note which is not part of the Instrument.

The reference number of the Instrument is SI 1995 No. 3297. Copies can be obtained from Her Majesty's Stationery Office (HMSO), and as always specialist advice should be obtained when applying or interpreting new laws.

Summary

1. Intellectual property rights (IPR) can be vital assets in a business.
2. IPR includes registerable rights such as patents, trade marks, and registered designs.
3. Unregistered IPR comprises copyright, design rights, trade secrets, goodwill and reputation. It is sometimes held that the right to prevent others from engaging in unfair competition is part of IPR.
4. Patent registration involves early disclosure, so consider the risks involved and the cost/benefit ratio. It is relatively costly to register a patent. To be patentable, inventions must have industrial application, they must be novel, and there must have been an inventive step in their creation. In the case of infringement, do you have the resources to sue?
5. A patent takes 2–3 years, but protection is retrospective to date of application. Protection is for 20 years.

6. Trade marks must be distinguishable from marks of other traders in the same class. Many popular names will have already been registered, so compile a list of choices. Protection is indefinite, for as long as registrations are maintained. It may be necessary to prove continued use to survive challenges from third parties.

7. Trade marks must be used to describe goods or services, not to define them. It is sometimes said that they should be used as adjectives but not nouns.

8. A registered design must be novel; it must be applied by an industrial process, appeal to the eye, and comprise pattern, shape, ornament or configuration.

9. Protection of registered designs is for 15 years, with compulsory licences after 10 years.

10. Citizens of the EU member states may establish unregistered designs. Protection lasts for 15 years.

11. Copyright may not be registered. It comprises the right to copy material which is itself original in that the author has not copied it himself. There are three classes of copyright with protection ranging from 15 years outright to 70 years after the death of the author.

12. Copyright involves the right to copy — just that. Concepts or ideas are not copyright. Provided there has not been systematic paraphrasing, a work with original language will be regarded as an original work.

13. Trade secrets must have commercial value, they must actually be secret within UK, and there must be a relationship of confidence between the parties for the secrets to be protected.

14. To establish a breach of confidence or trade secret ask three questions: (i) Was the matter actually secret? (ii) Was there a confidential relationship? (iii) Has the owner of the secret actually been harmed by the breach?

15. IPR may be exploited by outright sale for value or by licence. (It might also be exploited negatively by suppression on the part of the owner, in favour of a more lucrative alternative, but subject to certain anti-competition laws).

16. Licensing of IPR normally involves undertakings both by licensor and by licensee in order to be commercially viable.

17. Sub-licensing is possible, to many levels of secondary sub-licence.

18. Care is needed not to license more than the rights one has, and not to grant overlapping rights when one or more licences are exclusive.

19. Policing IPR infringements can be difficult, but against those who are caught the penalties can be severe.

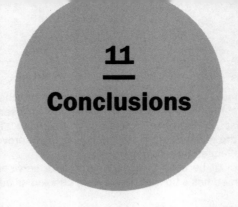

11
Conclusions

We have now surveyed the main steps necessary to establish control of the commercial and contracts function in our enterprise. We have surveyed the scene. We have designed and imposed control mechanisms.

We have considered the law of contract, and we have discussed easy and methodical ways of drafting agreements. We have reviewed 'boiler plate' clauses and we have buttressed our procurement routines by ensuring there is standard paperwork under proper control and with standard contract terms.

We have examined our risk patterns. We have considered ways of negotiating so that we can make the most of our business relationships both with customers and with suppliers.

We have reviewed sales of goods and services. We have even looked briefly at outsourcing. We have discussed the law of agency, and how it might affect our staff as well as our appointed distributors if we have any. We have also looked at intellectual property, its rights and the opportunities for exploiting them. What else is there to think about?

Let us consider two final points for review.

Keeping the team happy

You will not achieve all these things alone, unless your organisation is small. You will need a good team. Strive to surround yourself with the wisest people you can find, regardless of age, sex, formal qualifications, and even what other people tell you about them, unless you respect the judgement of those people. See each candidate yourself, and think carefully how you would work together. Does their perception of commercial matters coincide with yours? And how will they get along with your 'customers', both inside and outside the organisation?

If your unit has to be small, you can afford to make no mistakes. It may be that one of the biggest risks is in taking staff recruited from outside, who do not know their way around the company, nor the company culture. If you agree with this view, stick out for in-house recruits, and do not be over-influenced by personnel or Human Resources (HR) policies. If things go wrong, it will be *your* problem. You can only afford to take newcomers if you are to be given the time and resources to train them. Delegation has been described as 'the licensing of others to make mistakes on our behalf'. Too many mistakes in this area will not be tolerated!

Having recruited the best, how do you keep them motivated? To do this, your unit must become known as a stepping stone to higher office, not a home for 'dead-beats' who failed somewhere else in the hierarchy. Allow your staff to specialise, but not to the extent of having their usefulness atrophy.

One method is to run the unit like a firm of general practitioners in medicine, with yourself as senior partner rather than boss. Have each one specialise in a field of contract work, and let this be known to the other partners. After a while, each will refer special cases to him or her. Yet each partner still takes a turn of duty on the telephone or in the general office 'surgery', taking each 'case' through to completion whatever its constituent problems. Each one thus becomes known to, and respected by, the whole organisation. Make it known that you share ideas and expertise around the team, like good GPs, with 'case conferences'. This is one of the best and quickest ways of training contracts staff – far better than sending them on courses, though formal training has its place.

Like good general practitioners the unit must form links with its 'consultant surgeons', the specialist lawyers in public practice and other advisers with specific skills.

This approach works best with a centralised unit, of course, but there are ways of making it happen when you are geographically apart. It just takes more time, thought and effort.

Keeping the organisation briefed

In a dynamic company, people move. Roles and responsibilities change. Manuals of procedure get out of date, and despite the best of intentions they do not get amended.

We began with 'management by walking about'. Let us end with it too. Consider an annual 'contracts unit walkabout'. Plan a half-day 'road show'. Go everywhere. Offer talks or even videos on the law of contract and IPR. Make it fun. Invite audience participation. Have a problem-solving session.

Take it around the company. Do not only talk to senior managers. Get a list of the recently promoted project supervisors and invite them along too. The more august the company, the more complimented the newcomers will be. Make friends with them today, and they will be your supporters tomorrow.

Share your skills around. Get you and your team known as problem solvers, not people who put legalistic or bureaucratic obstacles in other people's way.

And finally . . .

If you do all the things in this book successfully then, as in the case of the inventor of the better mousetrap, your office will never be deserted and your telephone seldom quiet. But you will have *control*, and many people will not even realise it!

Appendix

Contracts management and the company secretary: a 'health warning'

It is not unusual for a company secretary to be invited to take responsibility for the company's contracts management or administration. There are many good reasons for it. The secretary frequently has legal, financial or commercial training. His work with the board of directors gives him an overall perspective in company affairs. He will be aware of business opportunities and risks as they are perceived at the very apex of the organisation, and he will frequently have lateral links with a good many other support services. The role of company secretary may not be a full-time one, especially within private companies and those which might be group subsidiaries. All these factors may be good reasons for a decision to combine the functions. Yet there can be dangers, and it is important that these are understood.

The role of the company secretary

Let us briefly consider the role of the company secretary. He is *de facto* the senior administrative officer of the company. It is to him that writs, summonses and other legal matters are addressed, and from whom prompt replies may properly be required. Some of these may be time-critical. As secretary to the board he is its servant and – to the extent that Cadbury procedures may require – the adviser to individual directors from time to time, upon matters which might need previous research on his part. Some of these matters might be quite urgent, and individual directors might well expect to be given a measure of priority reflecting what they may justifiably consider to be their seniority and responsibility within the enterprise.

The role of the contracts manager

Now consider the role of contracts manager. In many organisations the salesmen do the deals; the lawyers or contracts people get together later to settle the details. Frequently there is optimism among the sales staff that, because the decision makers have agreed and the sale has been closed, writing the contract will be mere routine. This may be the case. Often, however, it is not, and contract negotiations upon matters of supposed detail which can yet be sufficient to jeopardise profit, may stretch unexpectedly for many days. If the job is due to start they may become very urgent; and in the present economic climate, as never before, 'the customer is king'. The final stages of a crucial contracts negotiation may be no time for one of the principal negotiators to leave for a board meeting, or to answer a peremptory demand from one of the directors, however justifiable that demand may appear. For the time being, the company secretary has become a member of the front line sales staff, and everyone from the chairman down needs to be aware of it.

Resolving conflicts of priority

There are, of course, ways around this, many of which we address in this book. Deputies or assistants may be trained and appointed within either or both disciplines. Routines may be simplified. Relationships might be fostered with external law firms such that extra resources can be brought in as necessary. Care is needed, however, not to upset existing contract negotiations by changing the members of the team. Moreover external lawyers may not always have sufficient knowledge of the business and personal rapport with all of the directors to provide more than temporary cover for the appointed contracts manager or secretary, according to which role they are covering.

Each organisation will of course address these issues in ways that suit its individual needs. But addressed they must be, and every secretary needs to see that they are squarely faced at the outset. Otherwise, a One Stop Contracts Management programme might become a terminus – at least for the company secretary!

Bibliography

Black, H. C., Nolan, J. R. and Connolly, M. J. (1979) *Black's Law Dictionary* (St Paul, MN: West Publishing Co.) [probably the best law dictionary, albeit with a US bias].

Boyce, T. (1992) *Successful Contracts Administration* (London: Hawksmere) [a valuable text on the subject].

Fisher, R. and Ury, W. (1982) *Getting to Yes* (New York: Hutchinson) [the Harvard Law School Negotiating Project text].

Irish, V. (ed.) (1991) *Intellectual Property* (New York: McGraw-Hill) [manager's guide with illustrations; very readable].

Kennedy, G. (1985) *Everything is Negotiable* (London: Arrow) [how to negotiate and win; highly practical examples].

Melville, L. W. (1985) *The Draftsman's Handbook* (London: Oyez Longman) [one of the few books on this subject].

Napley, D. (1983) *The Technique of Persuasion* (London: Sweet and Maxwell) [a prominent litigation solicitor's view].

Nierenberg, G. I. (1973) *Fundamentals of Negotiating* (New York: Hawthorn/Dutton) [well known practitioner's psychological approach].

Philips, J. and Firth, A (1990) *Introduction to Intellectual Property* (London: Butterworth) [a readable book on a complex subject].

Reed, C. (ed.) (1993) *Computer Law* (London: Blackstone Press) [essential for those in the computer business].

Schmitthof, C. M. and Sarre, D. A. G. (1984) *Charlesworth's Mercantile Law* (London: Stevens) [a student text that has stood the test of time].

Treitel, G. H. (1991) *Law of Contract* (London: Sweet and Maxwell/Stevens) [right level of detail for everyday contracts matters].

Tunkel, V. (1992) *Legal Research* (London: Blackstone Press) [how to dig deeper if you have to].

Winkler, J. (1981) *Bargaining for Results* (London: Pan Books) [tactics and techniques].

Index

abstract of patent, 137
acceptance, 25–6, 44, 91, 114
   offer and, 24
access to site, 92
accommodation, 92
accounts payable, 66
Act of God, 55
addresses for communication, 55
administrative order, 60
administrator, 61
advertisement, public, 25
advice notes, 79
advisers, 89
agency, 10, 27, 42, 72, 91, 118, 124 *et seq*
agreement to sell, 110
agreements, collaboration, 7
algorithms, 47
allowances for contingencies, 93
Alternative Dispute Resolution, 54, 123
amalgamation, 60
ambiguity, 46
amendments to draft, 47
   order, 72
analysis of risk, 89
anti-social purposes, 136
anticipatory breach, 31
Anton Piller order, 147
appearance of goods, 111
appendices, incorporation of, 47
application, industrial, 135
Arbitration Act 1979, 54
arrangement with creditors, 60
art, 141, 148
articles of association, 24, 30, 124
assent, to deed, 23
asset distribution, 96
assignment, 59
attorney, power of, 124, 129

enduring power of, 130
audit, right to, 144
author's rights, 141
authority control, 18, 19
   of agents, 126
   Five Star Guide, 128

Back Burner, negotiating ploy, 106
background IPR, 137
backhanders, 129
bank guarantee, 41, 90
bankruptcy, 46, 60, 130
bargaining over clauses, 52
   strength, 111, 118
barter, 116
BATNA, 99
Battle of the Forms, 71
benchmark performance, 93
bid bond, 7, 25
   manager, 13
   number, 13
   team, 92, 94
blanket order, 69
board of directors, 18
   resolution, 128
boiler plate clauses, 28, 51
bonding, organisational, 121
bonuses, terminal, 90
breach, 21, 31, 32, 47, 76, 112
break clause, 77
breaks, time, 122
British Consulates, 91
British Standard, 73
broadcasts, 141
BS 5750, 94
budgetary estimate, 34
buildings, 9, 109
burdensome contract, 31

Business Interruption insurance, 86
business name, 38
business, core, 120
buy, or make, 66
buyer, 65, 115

c. & f., 69
c.i.f., 69
Cadbury.Code, 11, 12, 152
capacity, 127
care, 57, 116
carriage, 69, 113
case conferences, 151
case law, 22
cash flow, 41, 92
certainty of meaning, 27
    of terms, 24
Certificate of Incorporation, 127
certificates of conformity, 79
certificates of insurance, 94
change order, 32, 78, 122
Chapter 11 (USA), 61
chattels, personal, 109
checking invoices, 69
choice of jurisdiction, 52
choice of law, 52
choosing trade marks, 138
civil commotion, 55
clause analysis, 93
    headings, 45
    numbering, 44, 45
claw-back, 39, 74
codes of practice, 122
collaboration agreements, 7
collusion, 6
Commercial Agents Regulations 1993,
    130
commercial matters, 90
commission, 91, 129, 131
commissioning, 88, 114
common law, 21, 22, 32–34, 59
    wife, 125
communication, addresses for, 55
companies, 42, 38
Companies Act 1989, 24
company cultures, 89
    secretary, 24, 128, 152
compensation, 32, 117
competition, unfair, 140
competitive situations, 6
completion, 39
composition with creditors, 60
computer generated works, 141

software, 63
condition precedent, 31
conditional clause, 26
conditions, 31, 46, 110, 112
confidentiality, 79, 83, 91, 122,
    140
confirming orders, 6
conflicts of priority, 153
consequential loss, 57
consideration, 23, 28, 39, 123
consultants, 10, 30, 58, 89
consumers, 22, 25, 111, 112
contempt of court, 33, 34, 147
contingency allowances, 93
contract clearance, 16, 18
    implied by conduct, 28
    in writing, 28
    law, 1 et seq, 21
    management, 51
    number, 69
    of record, 23
    of service, 10, 30, 88
    risk, 87
    type, 13
    verbal, 28
contractor, 31
contracts manager, 153
    register, 13, 14
    road show, 151
    unit, 151
control, 11, 12
    of defence, 59
conveyances, 9, 21
copyright, 7, 63, 122, 140
Copyright Design and Patents Act 1988,
    141
Copyright Tribunal, 148
core business, 120
cost, 88
    of patent, 137
    of trade mark, 139
costing, 92
counter offer, 25, 26
court order, 33, 34, 61
court, friends of, 53
credit insurance, 75
    status, 4
credit, letters of, 90
crime, 30
criteria, performance, 122
critical path analysis, 39
cross referencing, 45
Crown use, 137

cultures, company, 89
customer specials, 95

damage, consequential or indirect, 57
damages, 31, 32, 41, 77, 110, 111, 115
  for delay, 41
  duty to contain, 33
  liquidated, 34, 37, 88
dealing as consumers, 112
death, 26, 111, 117, 130
  liability for, 58
declaration of war, 55
deed, 23, 24, 128
  of gift, 28
  poll, 28
defects, 75, 76, 111
defence, control of, 59
defined terms, 42
defining the parties, 41
definitions, 42, 44, 70
Del credere agent, 129
delegation, 150
deliverables, 39, 109
  staged, 63
delivered work, use of, 62
delivery, 65, 73, 91, 109, 113
  address, 66
  date, 31
  in instalments, 114
  of deed, 23
  time of, 110
Department of Trade and Industry, 91
description, 110
  of patent, 137
design rights, 7, 140
designs, 65
  registered, 139
diligence, 57, 58, 126, 129
directors, 10, 11, 24, 33, 34
Director General of Fair Trading, 119
discharge of contract, 30
  under frustration, 31
disclosure, 136
  by agent, 129
discounts, 93
dispute resolution, 123
District of Columbia, 53
divisions of large companies, 41
document muster, 10
documentation, 79
documents, precedence of, 56
domain, public, 142
drafting, 37

drama, 148
drawings, 65
duties of agent, 129
duty to mitigate loss, 33

early termination, 122
electronic document interchange (EDI),
  79
email, 16, 26, 56, 83
emergencies, contract starts, 16
employees, 10
employers liability, 86
employment contract, 30
encumbrances, 116
enduring power of attorney, 130
enemy status, 130
entire agreement, 60
entry, right of, 144
environment, 89
equitable doctrines, 22, 33, 34
  remedies, 33, 34
equity, 22, 32, 59
errors and omissions, 86
escrow, 144
essence of agreement, 27
estimate, budgetary, 34
estimating and planning, 92
etiquette for signing contracts, 48
European Council Directive
  No 93/98/EEJ, 148
European Union law, 30
evidence, extrinsic, 46
ex parte injunction, 33, 34, 147
ex works, 69
examination of goods, 114
exchange contracts, 116
  control, 91
  of letters, 71
exclusion clauses, 111, 112, 117
  of liability, 57
  of warranties, 29
exclusive licence, 143
execution, 39
expatriate staff, 91
expiry of notice, 47
exploiting intellectual property, 142
extrinsic evidence, 46

f.o.b., 69
facilities management, 120
facts, material, 129
failure to deliver, 76
failure to pay, 46

fair compensation, 32
  dealing, 118
  trading, 119
false description, 115
faulty goods, 114
faulty workmanship, 73
fax, 16, 26, 56, 83
Federation Against Software Theft, 140
felled timber, 109
fiduciary services, 10
figures and words, 46
films, 141, 148
final payments, 63
  test, 89
financial matters, 90
finish of goods, 111
fire officer, 9
fire prevention, officer, 9
fire risk, 86
fitness for purpose, 29, 73, 110
Five Star Guide, 128
flawed contracts, 29
flood, 86
flow charts, 47
force majeure, 31, 46, 55, 78, 81, 82, 93
foreground IPR, 137
Foreign & Commonwealth Office, 124
foreign exchange, 26, 91
forms, battle of the, 71
friends of the court, 53
frustration, discharge under, 31
fulfilment of contract, 30

general agent, 129
general terms and conditions, 46, 52, 56,
  60, 70
generic words, and trade marks, 138
gift, deed of, 28
global rights, 143
good faith, 116, 118
goods, 65
  inwards, 66, 94
  receivable, 6
  ownership of, 74
  sale of, 109
  unsolicited, 75
goodwill, 140
growing trees, 109
guarantees, 41, 90, 118

Harvard Law School, 98
headings of clauses, 45
heads of agreement, 28

help desk support, 10
horizontal marketing, 143

illegality, 60
immoral purposes, 136
implied agencies, 125
  by conduct, contract, 28
  terms, 110
impossibility of performance, 31
incapacity, mental, 130
incoming goods, 6
incorporating by reference, 44, 47
Incorporation, Certificate of, 127
indemnity, 57, 59, 75, 79, 80, 93, 130
indirect loss, 57
individually negotiated terms, 116
industrial action, 55
industrial property rights – see intellectual
  property rights, 7
inflation, 93
infringement, 79, 80, 145
injunction, 33–4, 147
injury, 58, 111, 117
insolvency, 46, 115
inspection, goods inwards, 94
  quality, 66
instalments, delivery in, 114
instruction to proceed, 17
instructions, taking, 37
insurable risks, 80
insurance, 10, 75, 84–6, 112–3
  brokers, 9
  certificates, 94
intellectual property, 7, 63, 122, 134
International Courts of Justice, 53
Internet, 56
interpretation, 46
invalidity, 60
inventive step, 135
inventors, 136
invitation to tender, 24, 25, 94
invoices, 6, 69, 79
inwards, goods, 66
ISO 9000, 94
items from stock, 74
  on loan, 81

job number, 13
joint ventures, 7
jurisdiction, choice of, 52

key people, 89
know how, 134, 142

land, 9, 28, 109
landlord and tenant, 9, 32
landlords' licences, 9
lapse, 26, 26
law library, 35
law, choice of, 52
lawyers, specialist, 151
leases, 9
legal code, 82, 90
    matters, 90
    relationship, 24
letters of credit, 90
    of Intent, 4, 16, 34
levels of authority, 128
liability, 57
    for death or injury, 58
libel, 21, 86
library, 35
licence, 63
licensing, 143
licensors, 63
lien, 114
limit of liability, 16
limiting liability, 77, 112
liquidated damages, 34, 77, 88, 93
liquidation, 46
liquidator, 47
literature, 141, 148
loan items, 81
loss of profits, 86
loss, indirect or consequential, 57
    mitigation of, 33, 48

made to order goods, 112
mail order, 25
maintenance, 10
make or buy, 66
Management by Walking About, 2
management consultants, 58
managing intellectual property, 145
manner of use, trade marks, 138
material facts, 129
mental incapacity, 130
mercantile law, 21
merchantable quality – see satisfactory
    quality, 29
milestones, 3, 88, 92
misleading statements, 115
mistake in contracts, 29
mistakes, rectifying, 48
mitigation of loss, 33, 48
money, retention, 91
moral rights of author, 141

motivation, 90, 150
motor insurance, 86
music, 141, 148

name, business, 38
necessity, agents of, 125
negligence, 21, 57, 58–9, 111
negotiating, 47–51, 98, 153
non-exclusive licences, 143
notary, 124
notice, 47
novation, 121–2
novelty, 135
numbering clauses, 44

objectives, 1, 92, 99
obtaining signatures, 48
offensive material, 136
offer, 88
    and acceptance, 24
offeree, 25
offeror, 25, 27
office accommodation, 9
    contents, 86
officers, 10, 33–4
omissions, and errors, 86
operating environment, 89
opposition to patents, 136
order amendments, 72
    numbers, 79
    of court, 33–4
    purchase, 66
orders, confirming, 6
organisational bonding, 121
original literature, 141
ostensible authority, 127, 132
outsourcing, 119
overs, and shorts, 66, 114
overseas contracts, 48
ownership of goods, 74, 112
ownership, transfer of, 121

packaging, 75
part consignments, 114
partnership, 38
passing off, 8, 138
patent, 7, 63, 122, 134–5, 145
payable, accounts, 6, 66
payment, stage, 32
    time of, 110
payments, final, 63
    stage, 40, 63, 90
penalties, 3, 93

performance, 31, 39, 93, 122
  specific, 33–4
perishable goods, 115
personal chattels, 109
  relationship, 129
  rights and obligations, 21
  service, 88
PERT, 92
planning and estimating, 92
planning sheet, negotiating, 101–5, 107
point of delivery, 66
  of sale, 113
policing rights, 146
political factors, 91
portfolio of risk, 95
possession, quiet, 116
  right of, 112
postal rule, 27, 56
power of attorney, 124, 129
  enduring, 130
practice, codes of, 122
PRAMKU test, 2, 88
preamble, 43
precedence of documents, 56
  of terms, 46
precedent, condition, 31
preconditions, 39
price, 39, 75
  list, 25
prime contractor, 31
principal, 124, 127, 130
principled negotiating, 98
priority, in interpretation, 46
  conflicts of, 153
privity of contract, 32, 58
procurement, 65
product liability, 86
production superintendent, 69
professional advisers, 89
professional skill, 58
profits, secret, 129
project log, 18
  manager, 13
  plan, 92
  risk, 87
promisor, 23
prompt payment, 6
property, transfer of, 112
proposal, 25, 88
protecting rights, 146
public advertisement, 25
  domain, 142
  interest, 30

knowledge, 79
liability, 86
publicity, 53
purchase order, 5–6, 51, 66, 69, 94
  requisition, 6, 65
purchaser, 25
purchasing, 5
  cycle, 65
  system, 68
purpose, fitness for, 29, 73, 110

quality, 73, 88, 94, 110
  assurance (QA), 95
  checks, 6
  control, 112
  inspection, 66
quantity, 6, 88
quantum meruit, 27–8, 77
quarantine store, 66
questionnaires, risk, 87
quiet possession, 116

ratification, 126–7
rating system, risk, 87
real estate, 9, 109
reasonable skill, 58
received unexamined, 66
receiver, 47, 61
receiving order, 60
recitals, 46
reconstruction, 60
recordings, sound, 141
rectification, 30, 76
rectifying mistakes, 48
  on site, 69
regional factors, 91
registered designs, 7, 135, 139
  intellectual property, 134
  office, 38
reject note, 67
rejection, 75
remedies for breach, 32
repair contracts, 116
repeated words, 46
repossession, 112
representation, 60
reputation, 140
requisition, purchase, 6, 65
resale price maintenance, 30
researcher's notebook, 145
resolution of disputes, 123
restraint of trade, 30, 131, 142
Restrictive Trade Practices Act 1976, 30

retention money, 91
return, sale or, 112
revocation, 26
right of entry, 144
    to audit, 144
    to inspect books, 131
riots, 55
risk, 5, 11, 18, 49, 51, 57, 74–5, 80, 84, 113
road show, 151

safety standards, 88
Sale & Supply of Goods Act 1994, 109
Sale of Goods & Services Act 1982, 109
Sale of Goods Acts, 22
Sale of Goods Act 1970, 29
Sale of Goods Act 1979, 73, 109
sale of land, 28
sale or return, 112
sales, 89
    contracts, 2, 3
    of goods and services, 109
    proposal, 25
    tax, 53
samples, 111, 116
satisfactory quality, 29, 110
sea transit, 113
seal, 9, 23, 28
seasonal trade, 30
secret agent, 132
    profits, 129
    trade, 140
security, 93–4
self insurance, 87
sell, agreement to, 110
sequestration of estate, 60
service marks – see trade marks, 138
services, 65
    sale of, 109
serving of notice, 47
set off, 64, 117
settlement, 74
shorts and overs, 66, 114
signatures to contracts, 48
simple contract, 17, 28, 109, 128
single source suppliers, 111
site access, 92
    preparation, 41, 113
skill, 57–8, 116, 129
skilled staff, 92
slander, 21, 86
software, 63
sole sources, 94

trader, 38
sound recordings, 141
sources of supply, 94
spares, 80
special agent, 129
    situations, 7
    terms and conditions, 46, 56
specialist lawyers, 151
specialists, 10, 30
specials, customer, 95
specific performance, 33–4, 77, 115
    terms, 46
    the, 70
specification, 65
spot checks, 5
spreading risk, 96
staff, 90, 92
stage payment, 3, 32, 40, 63, 90
standard clauses, 28
    contracts, 3–4, 51
    terms and conditions, 46, 51–2, 89
state-of-the-art, 63, 76, 95
statute law, 21–2, 28–30
statutory requirements, 82
Stewart Gill v. *Horatio Meyer & Co*, 1992, 64
stock items, 74
stop loss insurance, 87
store, quarantine, 66
sub-contractors, 26, 31, 82, 88–9, 93–4
sub-licences, 143
subject to contract, 25, 28, 34
submission of patent, 137
superintendent, production, 69
supplier, 66, 76, 82, 88–9, 93–4, 111
Supply of Goods & Services Act 1982, 58, 110, 116
support, 80
sureties, 25, 90
Swiss law, 53
SWOT analysis, 38
synopsis, 39

taking instructions, 37
tax, 21, 53, 91
techniques of negotiating, 98
telephone deals, 105
telex, 56
temporary cover, contracts, 16
tenant, and landlord, 32
tendering, 6–7, 26, 88, 93,
terminal bonuses, 90
terminating agencies, 130

telephone deals, 105
telex, 56
temporary cover, contracts, 16
tenant, and landlord, 32
tendering, 6–7, 26, 88, 93,
terminal bonuses, 90
terminating agencies, 130
termination, 46–7, 60–1, 76, 122
terms and conditions, 46
   defined, 42
   individually negotiated, 116
territorial licensing, 143
   protection, 135
testing, 63, 88–9, 92
third parties, 111
threshold of technology – see state-of-the-
   art
timber, felled, 109
time, 88
   breaks, 122
   of delivery, 110
   of payment, 110
   of the essence, 30–1, 69, 74, 77, 88, 93,
     110, 114
timetable of events, 39
title, 73–4, 80, 144
   warranty, 144
tort, 21, 30, 58–9, 138
total quality management (TQM), 94
Trade Descriptions Acts, 115
trade dress, 8
   marks, 7, 135
Trade Marks Act 1994, 138
trade secrets, 8, 140
trader, sole, 38
training, 151
transfer of ownership, 121
   of property, 112
   of risk, 113
   of undertakings (TUPE), 122
Treaty of Rome, 30, 145
trees, growing, 109
trespass, 21, 30
trip wire, 99
trust for creditors, 60
trustee in damages, 33
twenty–eighty rule, 5

typographical arrangements, 141

ultra vires, 30
unascertained goods, 113
understanding, 60
undertakings, 122, 144
unenforceability, 29–30, 60
unexamined goods, 66
unfair competition, 140
Unfair Contract Terms Act 1977, 22, 57,
   111
unfair terms in consumer contracts, 57,
   111, 116
unilateral bias, 117
unprofitable contract, 31
unregistered intellectual property,
   140
unsolicited goods, 75
unsound advice, 86
use of delivered work, 63
used in tables, 45

value, 28, 39
   analysis, 146
variation order, 3, 32, 60, 78, 122
VAT, 53
ventures, joint, 7
verbal contract, 28
vertical marketing, 143
void contracts, 29
voidable contracts, 29
voluntary undertaking, 39

waiver, 82
war, declaration of, 55
warranties, 29, 31, 46, 55, 60, 76, 110,
   115
warranting title, 144
where used tables, 45
win report, 15
witnessing, of deed, 24
words and figures, 46
words, repeated, 46
working environment, 89
workmanship, faulty, 73
works of music and art, 141
world rights, 143